A HANDBOOK ON PERSONAL GROWTH

47 REFLECTIONS

TO NAVIGATING THE PATHS OF PERSONAL GROWTH

BRAD MEIER

ISBN 978-9-69-239239-6
9 789692 392396 >

Visit the author at www.saturneditors.com/bradmeier

TABLE OF CONTENTS

INTRODUCTION

Everyone wants to make the best out of their life in one way or another. We wish to see to it that everything we are engaged in works out for us. Just as our desires differ, so do our definitions of success and accomplishment, which also vary to a far-reaching extent. What is most obvious is that there are several ways that various people choose to approach life, depending on what works for them. While many people may have apparent and attractive goals and aspirations, the challenge is that oftentimes, people like an understanding of how to effectively handle their goals and aspirations, which is a major setback to them in their journey to achieving what they want. This book is creatively coined for individuals willing to maximize their existence and make the best use of the things at their disposal, even when such things are not so much to achieve their goals and aspirations at any given time.

To me, the only thing that makes the difference between the greatest people in the world and any other average person is the decisions they make and the paths they take. One common mistake that most people make is that they often mistake the route that many opt for as the right route. But in fact, this is not always the case. The fact that there are a lot of people taking that route doesn't make it the correct route. This reminds me of one very popular quote: "Two roads diverged in a wood, and I—I took the one less traveled by, and that has made all the difference." R. Frost (The Road Not Taken). The truth is that sometimes the path that is least traveled by The one that looks dejected and lonely is all that will make all the difference, and this is one of the reasons why this book was constructed to give an accurate perspective on some of the neglected routes, uncommon ideas, and seemingly strange habits that can yield the best results if developed into a habit.

You are probably wondering what the motivation behind the title of this book, *47 reflections of Life*, is all about. When dealing with a book that aims to better your existence, the common idea that comes to mind is something like the regular and common 10 ways to do this, 100 ways to do that, or 101 ways to get things done, but because this book is not your regular self-help or life hack book, it undoubtedly has to go beyond the regular things that are all over the place. So, it is pretty simple. I didn't write the classic: the 100 things no one has ever told you, the 5 habits that will change your life, 101 ideas to improve your life, or something like that, which are the whole number in marketing and communication as a means of persuasion and attention-grabbing, and this should suggest to you that this book contains information that you cannot find randomly at any location.

So, unlike other books that use enticing titles and standard descriptions that will only catch your attention yet fail to deliver the expected results, this book promises nothing other than the simple truth from my discoveries that will aid and guide you on your journey towards self-development. So, I choose to launch you through the least traveled paths because I do not only believe, but I am certain that it will make a difference, or actually, it will make all of the difference. This book's pages are littered with not just examples but suggestions aimed at providing you with a precise understanding and an accurate perspective of the points explained under each outline.

So, rather than the usual long writing that subsequently bores you, particularly if you are not a regular book lover, I have utilized some efficient tools that will engage you through the course of reading. Thus, it relieves you of the boredom that ordinarily comes with reading an average book. I will talk to you through stories and anecdotes about abstract topics. I will use the oldest device in the world to talk to you about something else: the story, the fable. Myths, tales, novels, and fables are effective communication tools for abstract subjects.

After all, we all know that Frost, when he talks about the less traveled road, is not talking about the woods but rather most of the untaken paths and strategies that a regular person will build a habit around. As you read through the pages of this book, prepare to be enlightened on strategies that will help you achieve your goals and overall be a better person in the way you approach the things you are involved in and life in general.

MANURE

I have had a lot of free time in the morning lately. I often find myself becoming more reflective during these moments amid the dawn when nature and its inhabitants are just waking up to their call of duty. During these hours, I randomly select topics in the palace of my mind and ruminate on them. I'm taking advantage of these moments to keep fit by walking in my countryside. The more I look at the fields that transpire mist at dawn, the more I notice how nature wastes nothing, not even waste.

Nature is built or created in such a way that nothing is really lost at all. With my little background in science, I know that the first law of thermodynamics states that energy cannot be created or destroyed; it can only be converted from one form to another. This means that even when it visibly seems that the element in question has exploded or is long dissipated, that energy still lies somewhere, perhaps in the atmosphere, looking for a way to be converted into another form later. This is especially evident when potential energy is converted into kinetic energy and then back to potential energy. All around us are pointers to the fact that nature truly takes care of itself and lets nothing perish because, while it may not be all that euphoric or pleasant at the present moment, it works until it becomes profitable in the long run.

For example, think of manure, which is the result of animals' feeding. Manure has a repulsive odor and is offensive to breathing conditions. In fact, because of their offensive nature, man has created sewage systems to funnel the waste away from the abode of man. Yet, manure is essential as an aid to the enrichment of the soil and the development of the soil nutrients. The soil's fertility is strengthened when manure is applied, and the crops tend to blossom buoyantly, flourishing with the aid of what they have been endowed with. Then we ask ourselves, are things really as they seem? Although we consider it repellent, feeding life in the fields is very important. In short, something new can be born from waste. Even from the very food waste that we throw away in the yard after we are done, nature has agents that feed off it and break it down into compost that will increase the soil's fertility.

I remember watching the recent animated movie "Land of Luck," where the main character encountered so much bad luck that she had to find her way around. While searching for permanent good luck, she stumbled upon a horse who had once had bad luck and had thereby met the love of his life, a dragon. Even when she had the power to choose good luck for the rest of her life, she chose a balance between both because she hit an epiphany that not all bad circumstances yield negative results. She had to learn her way around it and live her life to the fullest.

The same is true of life's bad luck, setbacks, and disappointments like manure. We should learn not to waste even this waste of our existence but rather to use it as a fertilizer to continue to grow and fortify ourselves.

Let every little moment count. That you are currently in a bad position should not permanently condemn you to a moping state. From the bad situation you are confronted with, there is an opportunity to learn the lessons. Every moment, good or bad, should be learned in sober reflection because there is always a lesson to learn. You never can tell. During your moments of depression, you begin to develop new energy for vitality to live life. There is also another addition. You are equipped with novel knowledge on how to help others who later hit a brick wall with the same challenges you were once faced with.

Here, this is my wish. Maybe a lot of waste has accumulated inside you for years, difficult times, or even a single day. Whatever the disappointment, pain, or hurt you may have experienced, use them as fertilizer for the new course of your life.

SOMETHING IS BETTER THAN NOTHING

A few weeks ago, I was busy all day. Between work, family, and unexpected car problems, I arrived in the evening completely exhausted. Fatigue overtook me, and I was ready to retire fully for the day. I should have gone to train, but the thought of packing my bag, going out in the cold, and heading to the gym made me anxious. Who wouldn't be? It was extremely cold and uncomfortable to step out of the coziness of my home to undergo another hard training session after the week's struggles. Surely, I thought I could take some rest and perhaps check off other boxes on my bucket list for the day and take to lounging.

I was ready to get up off the couch and watch some brain-dead episodes on Netflix. There were already brimming movie ideas in my head and a ravaging desire to binge-watch some shows I had earlier missed and the newest movies being talked about. I deserved it (isn't that what we always tell each other?). Of course, after the struggle, I thought rest was what I deserved. Isn't rest, as they say, sweet after labor? If the laborer is truly worthy of his wages, surely I was in no danger by deciding to pay myself the wages of relaxation and rest.

At that moment, some still-on moth neurons made contact to bring out this simple idea in my head: something is better than nothing. This singular statement propelled me into a meditative state where I sought to draw out the wisdom contained in this simple but witty aphorism. What could it possibly mean? It meant that rather than laying lazily on the couch while feeding off junk and sipping on some drink that could, in the long haul, affect my general well-being, I could just engage in an activity that might not be indulging at the moment but would be beneficial. Instead of postponing the duty to another day when the relevance would have been outlived, and I would have been forced to add another measure that would have become extremely uncomfortable, wouldn't it be better if I did it now?

Even if I had only trained for one minute, it would have been better than not training at all. If little droplets were accumulated one after the other, soon a pool of water would form, and if the dripping continued, it could become a large body of water. Waiting until it is the perfect or convenient time may turn out to be the worst gaffe ever made. The time for comfort might never come because the body desires its comfort amidst plushness. The discipline available in us will scream for the better option of the two: something. The I-will-do-it-later syndrome affects some people so much that they keep postponing until the workload reaches an extent that they can't swish off in one stroke. They become overburdened in the long run when they finally find the moral resolve to complete the task.

Doing a task endows you with the ability to expand. Once you put in one hour today, you could find yourself doing one-and-a-half hours tomorrow. These sessions, bound by virtue of consistency, continue to expand and benefit you. So, rather than taking the easy route of doing nothing, why not take the path of doing something, even if it appears insignificant?

Upon realization, I grabbed my bag, hit the gym, and did the lousiest workout of my life. I was listless, at 10% of my possibilities, with continuous breaks, but I did it. At first, it didn't look like what I would do on a normal day, but at least I thrust in my energy dutifully.

In the shower, I felt the mental and physical fatigue slip away and the satisfaction rise. I had done something worthwhile.

THE WEEK OF THE "GIVEUPPERS"

At the beginning of every New Year or during the final weeks of the close of the preceding year, resolutions are always made to make up for the excesses or shortcomings of the previous year. The desire to do better, live better, and aspire to a higher display of morality, discipline, and conventional character causes many to outline their character bucket list, which is set to be achieved and continued. Surprisingly, the initial enthusiasm fades, and, with time, the submerged and repressed "vices" or shunned conduct or lifestyle emerge again and, in some cases, become sharper than previous conduct.

The third week of January is the week in which, statistically, most people "give up" their good intentions from the beginning of the year. After two weeks of fireworks, either for an unexpected event or for a drop in motivation, many people slowly slip into old (bad) habits, ready to make their usual promises again on the next "magic date" (usually the first Monday of September). There is the quick, fleeting self-forgiveness that comes with a pat on the back and a promise to keep the rules better next time, even though the thought of breaking the rules again isn't far away.

This happens because many of us are unwilling to accept a simple paradox: "To develop discipline and patience, we need both." Yes, you read that right: we continue to delude ourselves that there is some magic pill or secret strategy out there that can transform us (by magic and effortlessly) into Superman or Wonder Woman. We want a quick fix like the snap of a fairy's finger or twist of a wand, transforming Cinderella from the knave-type to a princess. Similarly, in some movies, the villain is depicted as having a brief conversation with the hero and heroine, during which he realizes his faults and surrenders to good character. Does this really play out in the real world? We think that the immediate desire to change transforms into reality just by mere wishes or that if it were a wishing well, we could just throw a coin in and walk off, whistling away idly with our hands in our pockets and our heads in the clouds. We prefer to tell ourselves this lie to not face the reality of things: that change is tiring, irregular, and slow. This means it is normal that fatigue makes us want to quit, that two steps forward can be followed by one (or maybe three) back, and that nothing really seems to change until suddenly everything changes.

It is common for people to always seek to see their progress report and smile when the progress is in leaps and bounds. However, we often forget that there are days when the change does not become very visible until we look back in time and see that giant strides have been made. So, when there seems to be no obvious progress report, some become discouraged altogether. Sometimes, the prospect of fulfillment becomes endangered when there are a few slips here and there, and they lapse into their old habits, resigning to fate, thinking, "Que sera sera."

Stop replaying in your head the scenes of transformation you see in movies ("Rocky Training," so to speak): there will be no motivating jingle to accompany your efforts and dreams that your transformation will happen overnight. You have to be disciplined, even if you have never had it in your life, and you have to be patient, even if you want everything immediately. Having a plan that works and works at your own pace is also healthy. Many people often cheer loudly at the possibility of change but have no plans to carry it out. This lack of a structured plan leaves them vulnerable to being beset by discouragements and disappointments. If you truly want to achieve abstinence and total freedom from some old habits, you need to have a plan that is personal to you and that you can use to monitor your development rate.

You cannot escape this universal law, but accept it, and no goal can escape you when you put your mind to it. Even when you slip back into it, pick up the gauntlet again. The change need not be drastic or come without relapse.

Endeavor to rise again when you slip. You can lay hold of it and possess it once you focus on it.

FORREST GUMP METHOD

My niece Madilyn starts each day knowing exactly what she wants to accomplish. For example,

Study 30 pages of history.

Study 30 pages of math.

Do a 1-hour workout in the gym.

Read materials in English for at least 1 hour.

Having established the daily plan, she starts working on her micro-goals, and every time she completes one, she acts like Forrest Gump during the running scene. That day, I don't really know why, but I decided to go for a run, so I ran to the end of the road, and once there, I thought I'd run to the end of town, and once there, I thought I'd run through Greenbow County. Then I said to myself, "Since I've come this far, I might as well run through the beautiful state of Alabama." And so I did. I ran through all of Alabama, and I don't know why I kept going. I ran to the ocean, and once there, I said to myself, "Since I have come this far, I might as well turn around and keep running." When I got to another ocean, I said to myself, "Since I've come this far, I might as well turn around again and keep running. When I was tired, I slept. When I was hungry, I ate. When I had to eat, well, I did it!"

Like the protagonist of the Hollywood movie, Madilyn "Forrest," every time she completes one of her "basic" activities, she says: "Well, since I've come this far, we might as well do a little more!" After completing the already highlighted tasks, she still has the energy to do more and maybe study ten more pages or do that extra exercise in the gym that she didn't want to do. This self-paced activity gives her the grace and speed to attend to the tasks in a piecemeal fashion, which is not enervating and burdening.

Thanks to the "Forrest Gump method," our effective reader is able to carry on with her commitments every day. Adopting this method has had many advantages for her:

Every day, she felt satisfied with having completed at least her "basic" activities.

She is more serene and calm, knowing that she is ahead of the weekly "schedule."

She is proud of herself for not being satisfied and taking a few more steps than necessary. By craving more, she can meet her targets faster. In short, she applied the philosophy of not putting too much iron in the fire.

Well, why not try this strategy? I, myself, have started testing it in the past few days.

Here are some things I have learned that may be useful to you if you decide to apply the "Forrest Gump method."

Don't overdo it! When making plans for your day, ensure you don't clutter your schedule with a thousand to-dos. Instead, choose what Madilyn calls "basic" activities: those MINIMUM goals you need to reach to feel satisfied with your day. When you finish them, you can then incorporate some more at your own rate.

You don't have to go to the ocean every day. Taking the extra step must be a free choice, not an obligation. There will be days when the extra effort is worthwhile and others when it is more important to recover your energy.

Focus on priorities. For the "Forrest Gump method" to really work, we must learn to put aside our unreasonable desire to accomplish 1,000 different things. The focus must be on a few really important priorities.

In short, this trick is extremely effective when we trigger a virtuous circle that allows us to reach (and exceed) a few "minimum" goals every day, which really make a difference in the quality of our work and lives.

ROUTINE

The concept of routine (or habit) generally arouses two visceral responses. There are those who literally feel suffocated at the idea of having their life marked by habits repeated identically every single day, and there are those who find a sense of peace and control in their daily routines. Is the first or second right?

Both sides probably have something to learn from each other.

Having too many rigid routines risks emptying our lives of meaning, turning them into a sequence of robotic actions repeated ad nauseam. The activities may utterly lack meaning or be devoid of relevance because we have relegated them to something done by rote and nothing more. The activities bear no significance, and the rigidity makes them boring and just one more task to get rid of and tick off the to-do list as soon as possible. At the same time, living for the day as late 19th-century romantic poets did not necessarily contribute to our creativity and satisfaction; and precisely on the subject of "routine and creativity," I want to offer you an alternative point of view.

Many of us believe routine kills creativity, but how do you explain then that some of the most prolific artists, writers, and thinkers of the last few centuries were addicted to routine? Let's see some examples.

The great philosopher Immanuel Kant was efficiently personified. He lived his entire life in the small town of Königsberg and was so methodical and routine that his neighbors could synchronize their clocks just by looking at him. He always woke up at 5:00 sharp every morning, worked on his essays for exactly 3 hours, and then taught at the university for another 4 hours. After having lunch in his usual restaurant, at 3:30 pm, he set off for his usual walk in the park. He returned to dinner with a friend of his (always the same) and then went to sleep at 22:00. Even though he used this almost suffocating method (or maybe because of it), the German philosopher was one of the most prolific and important thinkers of the 18th century.

What about the Japanese writer Haruki Murakami, author of the splendid Norwegian Wood? In the months he devotes to writing a new book, Murakami follows a strict "athletic-literary" routine. He wakes up every day at 4:00 am and writes for at least five or six hours to complete at least ten new pages. In the afternoon, run 10 km or swim 1500m. Back home, after a shower, he reads or listens to music. At 9:00 pm, he was already in bed. Interviewed on the subject, the Japanese novelist said that following this strict daily routine helps him get into a kind of creative trance. Respecting this precise sequence of habits for periods that can last six months or a year has also helped Murakami develop a physical and mental strength reflected in every page of his novels.

So, should we also develop such rigid routines to cultivate our creativity and achieve our most ambitious goals?

No, not necessarily.

Even the most beautiful painting in the world can be confused by the background if it is not properly enhanced by the right frame.

Do not underestimate the power of routines; they do not kill your creativity and deepest nature. On the contrary, they can help you to fully express your potential. Some of these routine actions aid our creativity as we repeat them because they allow us the bliss of reflecting more and deriving inspiration. For instance, Immanuel Kant's creativity may have been cocooned in his interactions with his students at the university. Routines sometimes allow you to see a newer, fresher perspective on something you are otherwise used to doing with a lackluster mindset.

Similarly, routines aid in proper time management and help accomplish tasks and goals on time. That same act can be replicated in the process of doing one's job too.

If in this period you feel that you are wasting a lot of energy without making real progress, start thinking about how you can introduce some small habits that give more structure to your day. That way, you can enjoy your tasks better and give them enough space.

THE PALE BLUE DOT

Whenever I see a photo of the Earth seen from space, I think of this piece by Carl Sagan, "*That Pale Blue Dot*": "Look at that dot again. It's here. It is home. It is us. On it, everyone you love, everyone you know, everyone you've ever heard of, all human beings who have ever existed have lived their own lives. The sum of our joys and sorrows, thousands of religions, ideologies, and economic doctrines, so self-confident, every hunter and gatherer, every hero and coward, every creator and destroyer of civilization, every king and plebeian, every young couple in love, every mother and father, every hopeful son, inventor and explorer, every preacher of morality, every corrupt politician, every 'superstar,' every 'supreme commander,' every saint and sinner in the history of our species has lived there, on a tiny speck of dust suspended in a ray of sunshine. The Earth is a tiny stage in a vast cosmic arena. For me, it underscores our responsibility to look after each other more kindly and to preserve and protect the pale blue spot. It's the only house we've ever known."

The beauty of nature cannot be over-emphasized. It is the only place we have ever known and called home, and it is populated by humanity. Somehow, humans have made it to the top of the hierarchy and have dominated this planet for quite a while. Despite the various conflicts over race, gender, and other social and non-social constructs, humanity is still viewed as one. This is similar to the Ubuntu philosophy common to the African people. While the words are of African origin, they represent a concept that transcends the confines of African culture;

they delve deeply into one of the most fundamental concepts all societies cling to in holy awe. The concept of shared humanity is not alien to many communities. This is why humans remain inextricably linked to the Earth despite tribal, racial, sexual, and national differences. There are about three things to note from Sagan's short speech: the shared connection of humanity and the resultant duties and responsibilities, the duty of protection and preservation of the Earth, and the ability to see beyond the immediate.

The shared connection of humanity makes it a deliberate imperative to care for the inhabitants of the Earth. When you appreciate the beauty of nature and remember how during your first faltering steps of childhood, you had to be ferried across by someone somewhere and that we all need each other, then you will see no other reason not to render your help or support to anyone despite your differences. Nature itself is connected in so many ways that harm to one could be harm to all. This is why you must often remember that you are a speck in the midst of a giant entity and must do your bit to make life livable and enjoyable for the people you meet.

Our protection of the Earth and its natural resources will be informed by our early realization that this Earth is for humanity, and once it is destroyed, there is nothing else to bequeath as an inheritance to the humanity coming after your generation. We must endeavor to keep this home that we have always known to be safe, secure, and habitable for the succeeding generation.

Our ability to see beyond the immediate will keep us from appreciating the very reason for our existence on this beautiful planet. While we are not always visible on that map of the Earth, we know that we can take a bird's-eye view of the Earth and, for a moment, forget all the challenges that militate against our survival. Then, we can breathe a sigh of relief and appreciate the fact that we are participants in this whole stage and that we must play a positive part.

That's why I love to change my point of view when I'm too busy with problems and worries. I like to imagine being able to get up and fly into the deep cosmos.

Viewing that faded blue dot from this perspective helps me put everything back into perspective.

NINETY-TWO PERCENT

95% of adults go to sleep or wake up thinking about something that worries them. These worries may range from personal insecurities to anxieties and other thoughts that give them cause for concern. Of this chaos of things that worry us and continually carry on our shoulders, 40% will never happen. Good news or bad news? This means that almost half of our worries have no possibility of happening at all, yet we worry about them because we think they will happen. Perhaps because it has happened to those close to us or those we respect, we think we could be the next victims.

30% of these worries have already happened! But we keep reliving these happenings in our head torture-style video from A Clockwork Orange. This shows that almost half of the matters we worry about have already happened and may likely not bring any repercussions anymore. It is like beating a dead horse. There is loss in two ways: loss of energy which is definitely unfruitful and will not douse tensions but rather aggravate them and lead to loss of time, which could have been invested in other things and may have yielded considerable growth and development. If they had already happened, why bother about them anymore? This is caused by fears of reprisals or regrowth. Seeing patterns may unnerve you, causing you to quake at the happenstance of that same uneventful circumstance. In fact, sometimes, you see your fears come true in the lives of other people, and you begin to get the idea that perhaps yours is not too far behind.

Now, 12% are minor health problems such as a simple headache, which we tend to exaggerate (often also due to Dr. Google). This is becoming increasingly common because of the misinformation and disinformation that grows wild by the day. The ridiculous amounts of health ads targeted at consumers on social media are enough to instill fears in the hearts of people. 10% are minor nuisances (e.g., what shoes should I wear this morning?). 8% are real problems.

In practice, we devote enormous mental energies to 92% of worries that are technically called … BITCH! Yet that 92% of imaginary worries actually ruin our lives. They do it by taking away our serenity and sometimes even sleep! The effect of the statistics is to show us that far less than 10% of what holds up the vacuum of our minds as worries are actually something worrisome, whereas we devote much of the space of our mind to such worries. Hence, we see that worries are actually not really worth worrying about because they only become weights that we carry about mentally, and they cause us to lag behind in our duties and schedules. Instead of focusing our energy on something very productive, we spend the day finding ways to solve what we believe are problems and deserve attention. The reverse effect is that while we labor at them to find solutions to them, they do not really require any solution but just little adjustments that will give our hearts and minds the liberation they deserve.

Of course, knowing these stats won't help us magically make these worries disappear, but maybe it will help us get a new perspective the next time we suspect a brain tumor due to a mild migraine. Only then can we confront our problems better and stop being paranoid about so much as having a cold and attributing it to something it isn't. The truth is that the fear itself is lethal enough to kill because you are at risk of being exploited, or you become more susceptible to diseases since your defenses are down.

These stats are pointers that we should take life easy as it comes, and we do not need to almost beat ourselves up and tear our hairs out over every single issue. Through this, we can overcome our fears better.

PS: What about you? If you were to be objective, what percentage of your concerns is a real problem?

COAST TO COAST

Imagine leaving with a friend of yours for the adventure of your life to the United States, walking across almost 5,000 km from the Pacific Ocean to the Atlantic Ocean, crossing deserts, mountain ranges, and endless plains. You both leave from the sunny beaches of San Diego and meet at West Quoddy Head Lighthouse in the state of Maine. In fact, you have decided to embark on the journey alone, each at your own pace.

As you prepare for the course, you decide to follow a steady pace, completing 32.2 km (20 miles) every day. On the first day, you arrive just outside San Diego; on the second day, do another 32.2 km. On the third day, you enter the desert that stretches between California and Arizona. It's hot as hell, over 40 degrees, and all you want to do is rest in the cool of a shadow but keep going until you complete your daily 32.2km. You do the same in the following days.

As you enter the US hinterland, the weather begins to cool, a pleasant breeze blows behind you, and you could easily travel 40–50 km a day, but save your energy and continue with your steady pace. You arrive in the mountains of Colorado and find yourself in the middle of a snowstorm and wind, with temperatures well below freezing. The idea of holing up in your tent is very tempting, but you decide to get up anyway: you have 32.2 km of walking in front of you, not one less.

Finally, you reach the Great Plains; it is spring, and you walk surrounded by the scents of nature. Your pace is light; you grind kilometers effortlessly but still remain focused on your goal: 32.2 km a day, not one more. Time a few weeks at a steady pace, and you'll finally see the West Quoddy Head lighthouse illuminated by a glorious sunset. You did it; you arrived at your destination.

Going back a few weeks, on the day of departure, when you are both still in San Diego, your friend chooses instead not to follow a set plan but rather to organize himself from day to day, based on his physical condition and weather conditions.

Excited by the journey that awaits him, he travels more than 60 km on the first day, immediately arriving at the edge of the desert. The next day, he wakes up exhausted and completely soaked in sweat. He decides to wait for the temperatures to drop; they will recover in the following days. He maintains this erratic pace as he travels across the western United States; when the weather is good, he travels dozens of miles; when the weather is bad, he stays holed up in his tent, complaining.

Shortly before arriving in Colorado, he takes advantage of a beautiful day to cover almost 75 km but is swept away by a snowstorm at the end of the day, when he is now destroyed by exhaustion. He falls ill and stays in the tent for several days, waiting for his condition and the weather to improve. When spring finally arrives, weakened and dazed, it begins to descend towards the Great Plains. He can't even make it to Kansas City when he finds out you're already waiting for him at West Quoddy Head Lighthouse.

Discouraged, he continues his march, reaching you after several days.

The Principle of the 20-mile (32.2 km) Walk is a fictional story inspired by a passage from Jim Collins' book "*Great by Choice,*" in which, among other things, the principle of the 20-mile walk is explained. (32.2 km).

For years, Collins and his colleagues have analyzed hundreds of companies in search of the critical success factors that distinguish excellent companies from just mediocre ones. From these analyses, it emerged that the ability to stay focused on a single measurable goal and carry it forward consistently, despite adverse external conditions, is undoubtedly one of the elements that most make the difference between individuals, teams, and extraordinarily successful companies and individuals, teams, and companies that are lagging behind. Whether you are a student, a professional, or an entrepreneur, if you really want to achieve your most ambitious goals, you cannot leave them at the mercy of your internal conditions (e.g., motivation) or external ones (e.g., an unexpected event). If you continue to behave erratically, alternating study/work marathons with prolonged periods of fancazzismo, distraction, and listlessness, you will find yourself continually exhausted and late.

Instead, choose your 20-mile march; that is, stay focused on a specific daily target that can constantly bring you closer to your goal, and commit to reaching it every single day, despite everything and everyone. Choose how many pages to study each day and complete them at whatever cost. Choose how many kilometers to run every morning and grind them whether it's raining or the sun is shining. Choose how many customers to contact each day, and do not leave the office until you have made the last call.

The point is that we can't control our professors. We cannot control our colleagues. We cannot control our customers. We cannot control our competitors.

We can't control the weather. Heck, we can't even control our thoughts! But we can control our actions and decide what we choose to commit to each damn day.

So, choose your 20-mile gear and wake up every morning knowing that whatever happens, you will cover those fucking 32.2 km, not a meter less.

ENJOY LIFE

This week I want to talk to you about a topic that, as good and ambitious and always oriented towards achieving new goals as we are, we often forget. Learn to enjoy life more! I would know how to enjoy life more! A nice exotic trip, a dinner at a star restaurant, a new car, a vacation away from the daily work schedules, and the opportunity to spend time with family during this period will be more than enough to enjoy the fleeting moments of life and alleviate our worries.

There is only a small problem! To do all these things, you need time and money, and you never have enough of either one or the other! Let's not fool ourselves; those with the luck (or the skill) to have time and money certainly have more chances to enjoy life than those who work all day to take home a small salary. Yet it is not so automatic. In fact, there is an aspect that many underestimate, and that proves to be fundamental to truly appreciate our existence (regardless of how much we earn). Admit it, have you thought about gratitude? Have you truly graciously reflected on your existence, how far you have come, overcoming all the odds against you, and how you have improved in character and charisma over the years?

Well, that certainly doesn't hurt, but I wanted to talk to you about another element today. To enjoy life more, we must learn to pay more attention to the moments that make us feel good. Yes, you read that right. Our perception of reality is often subjective, and past experiences are often filtered (and distorted) by fallacious memory. If we continue to focus on moments of difficulty, discomfort, and sadness while neglecting those of pleasure, happiness, and lightheartedness, we can hardly enjoy life, don't you think? If we allow the impenetrable fog of the bad moments to becloud our optimistic sense and linger in our minds, then we do ourselves a great disservice because we will not learn to appreciate the moments of celebration, joy, and euphoria that we have had. In other words, our minds will be incarcerated in that arena of gloom, and we will live our days constantly reminded of the gloom of life.

Here is a simple, practical strategy to appreciate our days more:

Every day, write down an experience, even a small or brief one, which has remained particularly ingrained in you, something you want to fix in your memory, a moment of yours. You have led a successful life.

Also, make sure to celebrate your little wins. No matter how minor, do well to pat yourself on the back and remind yourself that you are better than you were before. Your wins matter to you; they give your self-esteem a new turn by creating a solid floor for your self-esteem to germinate on and flourish. Even

As the weeks go by, repeating this little habit daily will help you change your perception of your life. You will then notice that it is not necessarily the money that gives the joy, but the fact that you think you have done a good job makes it well-deserved for you to take some time off and celebrate yourself. It doesn't need to be extravagant. Extravagance is not an assurance of the enjoyment of life. It only adds its perks to the real deal. In whatever profession or state you are in, learn to enjoy your life at your pace.

Well, it will help you enjoy your life more.

Of course, if you are already in the habit of writing a diary, you can safely add two lines to your daily pages.

Remember, nothing complicated; just try to notice something that makes you feel good every day; the more you try, the more these episodes will appear in your days. Today, create your own testimony and enjoy your life better.

RESISTANCE

For some months now, I have decided to end my daily shower by staying at least 2 minutes under frozen water. No, don't worry, I'm not crazy! As out of place as it may sound, it is geared towards a particular purpose.

Numerous studies on the benefits of "cold showers" (the "cold showers") and cold therapy have recently returned to the fore, also thanks to personalities like Wim Hof. Yet my choice is not dictated (only) by health reasons. Those 2 minutes a day under frozen water are, for me, above all, a mental workout, a real gym for

my willpower, and a raw test for the flexibility and tenacity of my strength and tolerance.

In fact, I hated every single cold shower I had done so far. Every day, before turning the knob towards the intensely blue area, my mind began to make dozens of rationalizations: "Come on, today is not the case. It will be a heavy day; you deserve at least the pampering of a hot shower." "In the end, you can get the same benefits even if you don't do them all every day." "Maybe today we make it lukewarm. What do you say?" These excuses gush up into my mind at the mere trembling of my body immediately after the water hits hard. It would have just been easy to quit and admit that I needed some warmth, after all.

These avoid-cold-shower rationalizations are a prime example of what Steven Pressfield calls the "Resistance," that is, that cosmic force that constantly operates in opposition to our realization. The "resistance" has a single mission: to preserve the status quo, and it is willing to use any means to ensure none of us makes our dreams come true. It tapes the comfort zone with a "Do Not Cross" warning sign and urges us to stay within close comfort.

The "resistance" can, in fact, present itself in the form of rationalizations (my Achilles' heel), fears, anxiety, distractions, and doubts. No matter what dress it decides to wear, the "Resistance" will continue to fascinate or attack us until it has achieved its goal: to hinder our change. So, instead of developing a thick skin that can help us combat and face life with a sharp tenor, our body and mind want not to resist but take life as it happens. Rather than build our confidence and resolve, we tend to compromise and surrender to the wiles of this resistance.

In the moments preceding the shower of frozen water on my skin, the "Resistance" drops its mask. I can clearly see it acting in my thoughts, and every time I notice it, I turn that damn knob. It wants me to shy away from doing what would harm it. That cringing effect, in fact, spurs me to get it done away with as soon as I can, and then I turn that knob.

Dealing with the "resistance" is never pleasant, and it never becomes easy, but every time we stand up to it, we get a little stronger and our dreams a little more real. We find out that we can have the enthusiasm to do it next time.

Here, when my "torture of the cold" comes to an end, I am often inundated by a pleasant warmth, a warmth that arises in-depth, arising from the awareness that the "resistance" will continue to trap me for the rest of the day, but that I will be able to recognize them and turn the "knob" in the direction of my will each time. Thus, my will is truly under my control, and not even the fleeting moments and ephemeral events can have their say in my decisions.

This week, I also wish you to face the many incarnations of the "Resistance" and to be able to recognize and defeat it every single time. The only way to overcome this would be to recognize that "Resistance" and douse every single flicker of light it rears in the direction of suggesting what shouldn't be to you.

WHAT'S YOUR EXCUSE?

A few weeks ago, I decided to spend a relaxing weekend in Bath, a lovely English town famous for its thermal springs, also appreciated by the ancient Romans. On Saturday mornings, I go to Paddington Station. I'm 10 minutes early, so I decide to sit in front of the time monitors.

Train canceled.

At one point, an elderly gentleman approaches, holding the inevitable tea in a cardboard glass. He sits next to me and starts talking to me like this, without much preamble. A whole tirade begins about the misadventures of his glasses (they are visibly fixed to the good and better with the scotch). They taught me to be courteous to everyone, but honestly, at 8 am on Saturday, after finding out that my train was canceled, I'd rather listen to Alec Benjamin than the specifics of the different frames and the cost of replacement lenses!

I can't take another two minutes of Shuron teleshopping. I'm about to come up with an excuse to walk away when I casually ask the gentleman where he is going.

"Ah, I just got back from Australia; I go camping every year for three months. There's this place south of Perth with some spectacular waves!" To which I replied: "Ah, she likes to breathe the sea air! But why does she travel all the way to Australia when a vacation on a Mediterranean island would be more comfortable and relaxing?"

"But young man, how can I then surf?! The currents coming from Antarctica create perfect waves!"

And I was utterly shocked.

John (this is his name), at the age of 70, played solo every year to do three months of wild camping and surfing in one of the most remote areas of Australia, with waves of several meters. Starting my weekend with this "wake-up marmot" chat made me realize that we tell each other a lot of lies and excuses about what we can and cannot do.

I do not deny that there are real limits with which many of us inexorably collide; however, many other limits exist only in our little heads, and we hold them too tightly because letting them go would mean facing an uncomfortable truth: in the end, we are the architects of our destiny, and if we are currently on the point of this path called life that we do not like, the responsibility for change is ours and ours alone.

So, I have only one question for you this Monday morning: What's the excuse you often tell yourself for not chasing your dreams?

Many of us give diverse excuses as justifiable reasons for our inability to fulfill our mandates. It seems comforting, at times, for us to point away from ourselves to excuses as the why for our unsatisfactory conditions. Apart from the gratification, it makes us shun responsibility, and we can generate sympathy from all quarters by people sending in their wishes and goodwill. Sometimes, we just do not want the hard, cold, and bitter truth that we are part and parcel of the negative goings-on in our lives, and we blatantly refuse to admit the truth that we are responsible for our present state. The truth is that the same scenes we recognize as obstacles may cease to be so in another context. For instance, were Elon Musk to call on a very rainy day for you to visit Silicon Valley and get your dream Tesla ride, the weather conditions could easily be ignored. Yet, the same weather could be used as an excuse at a less favorable moment.

This is not to say that all excuses are unjustified. It only brings to the fore the fact that some of our excuse-making attempts could be quashed, and we could take responsibility for our actions and inactions. Change is only possible when responsibility is involved. It is time to let go of the "comfortable" reasons for not following your dreams and take charge.

BECOME A BILLIONAIRE

Become a billionaire.

When faced with large numbers, our minds (which tend to reason linearly) get a bit confused. Take, for example, the difference between $1 million and $1 billion. We know for a fact that $ 1 billion is a lot of money, but so is $1 million, right?

So, let's try understanding the difference with a simple thought experiment. Imagine replacing each $1 with a second of time. At this point, we will have 1 million seconds, which is about 11 days; 1 billion seconds, corresponding to about 32 years. Now the difference is much more obvious, right?

Considering this comparison, imagine that an old billionaire, now close to death, is willing to pay you $1 for every second of your life. Specifically, he proposes to buy 32 years of your life in exchange for $1 billion. If you accepted, he would instantly rejuvenate 32 years, and you would instantly age by the same number of years. Would you be willing to accept this exchange?

If your answer is "No," you will agree with me that, in fact, many of us are already billionaires, time billionaires, yet we rarely appreciate this richness, continuing to waste our days. That is why, today, I would like you to think of that old, decrepit billionaire ready to suck your life at any price. Just like you see business magnates, brokers, and investors do in the markets, time is an investment bound to yield future interest. No matter what form your investment may take, whether good or bad, the basic principle is that you will reap what you sow. The type of investment you sow into the period ranging between planting and harvesting is determined by how much you honor your time. Time is one of the gifts of nature that man can barely pay for till the day of death. This is because time is willed by a force beyond the capacity of humanity, and within that space called time, you are allowed to act on the stage of the world any way you wish: villainously or heroically. It is all up to you.

Take, for instance, the reason why the billionaire is willing to buy some of your time. Why do you think he would want to? He knows that time has an inestimable value and that the whole gamut of his wealth only features in the realm called "time." Without it, his wealth has no place in it, and he is as good as being without it. So the question is, have you realized the value of your time? If so, what do you do with it, knowing full well that your current actions—and inactions—will determine the trajectory of your life, and it may even affect the lives of others? Because you have control over your time, you can spend it however you want. Be reminded that your time remains your greatest asset and that you were gifted with it.

So today, have a deep rethink and ask yourself how fairly you have been using your time, either to assist others or to do otherwise. If the self-examination does not turn out the best results or you find lapses in the way you have used your time, it is best to redirect your steps and begin a new course, charting a new path for the future and a beacon for others to follow. Great men and women have lived in time, using their time well, and history has exonerated them for the positive use of their time while on this planet. It is up to you to do the same.

If you turned down their offer, remember why you did it—honor your time.

EARN MONEY WITH YOUR PASSIONS

It will be 10-15 years that the Internet has been haunted by articles, videos, advertisements, and various info-products sharing the same tired formula (presented in different sauces): "Find out how to earn with your passions!" It is impossible to remain impassive in the face of such a succulent promise that comes with monetary incentives. In a job market where 40% of young people can't even get in, and 80% of that hate what they do inside, the idea of being able to make money with their hobbies is seen as the Holy Grail, the only way they can do two things at a time: develop their passions and also turn them into a goldmine of sorts where they can rake in anywhere from mid to high profits.

What other idea could sound better? Social media is flooded with many engaging clickbait articles of this sort, which sell themselves off as being quick and sure ways to monetize one's passions and make a profit. People feed on these humongous contents and begin to act on them, but some later get discouraged when it turns out that they have little or no turnover of profits.

Well, I don't hide from you that I, too, more than ten years ago now, pursued this glittering promise. During this time, I've been fortunate to achieve some positive results, but more importantly, I've learned what it truly means to earn a living from your passions. Here, what I will tell you will be a little different from what the various para-gurus imply. On the other hand, you will not have to shell out $

1,997 (limited places!) to find out.

So, the first point is to stop trying to make money with your passions. In fact, stop looking for your passions. Being obsessed with the idea of having to find your passions and maybe even having to monetize them is the wrong way to do the wrong thing. That sounds like starting on the wrong footing, to begin with. The very thought of flipping your passions for coins is detrimental to the entire gospel of building passions. When money becomes the motive for a passion, it is easier to derail from the true reason for pursuing passions. Instead, learn to master any skill (at first, it doesn't matter as much as many believe). It may not even be something you love, but it must be something where you feel you can become the best in the world. Once you become a "black belt" in this area, you will have the opportunity to dedicate your time to those work activities you enjoy most, leaving the others to new colleagues, collaborators, or competitors. Persevering in this spiral of excellence, you will finally find yourself spending your days doing what you really love (which is nothing more than the very definition of passion), and you will be rich when you thoughtfully do it.

So I repeat: stop trying to understand what your passions are or how you can transform them into the business of the third millennium. Start getting your hands dirty, step into the arena, work day after day to become the best in the world in your field, and then enjoy the fruits of your effort. Earning while following your passion is a promise as tempting as it is misleading. On the contrary, pursuing the path of excellence is certainly less tempting (indeed, it is damn tiring), but it is the only high road to live (and live well) by doing what you have learned to love and not to love "in theory," but in daily practice.

GET WHAT YOU CAN TRADE

A few weekends ago, I attended an interesting training course in Orlando. Also among the speakers was an Israeli negotiation expert. During his speech, there was a sentence that particularly struck me: "In life, you do not get what you deserve, but what you negotiate." And the more I reflect on this phrase, the more I find it applies not only in business but also in our personal lives.

The inevitability of this truth quickened my consciousness to what exactly he had meant by the words "negotiation." I'm not just talking about the "negotiations" we have with our friends, family, or partners, I'm talking about the negotiations we have every single day with ourselves. At the center of all decisions and all that revolves around us, we play a key role because of the very negotiations and deals we strike with ourselves. Perhaps an explanation would do.

We all deserve to make our dreams come true. God forbid, but deserving it is insufficient: we must constantly bargain with ourselves about our motivation, procrastination, and fears. The concept of what is truly deserving may not always be the subject of discourse. This is because, despite all that we may truly deserve, we need to constantly and consistently up our games by negotiating with ourselves on what steps to take and what not to take.

In fact, more and more studies in the field of neuroscience are showing that what we perceive on a conscious level as a unique and integral personality (the voice in our head) is actually nothing more than the result of incessant negotiations between different parts of our brain. Sometimes, the pre-frontal cortex wins (more logical and rational); other times, the limbic system wins (governed by primordial emotions), and so on (the interaction is much more complex, of course). The outcome of these negotiations will determine what we really get in our lives.

So, if you haven't gotten what you want yet, try asking yourself what you need to negotiate differently with yourself to get it. Maybe you need to come to terms with your fears by gradually putting one foot out of your comfort zone and giving yourself a well-deserved rest. Maybe you need to find an agreement with the laziest part of you, defining a realistic study/work plan which you can and must respect rather than a perfect but unachievable plan. The number of negotiations we must regularly have with ourselves to accomplish a set of objectives is multitudinous. We must jerk ourselves from our characteristic slumber or mental acedia and make solid plans to keep us one step ahead of our current state. These negotiations must continue to address the very undercurrents of our lives. Speaking to ourselves, we must also arm ourselves with the needed knowledge to resolve every bit of our dilemma. As we continue to negotiate with ourselves and make resolutions that we follow and keep, we will notice a new level of change. Maybe you only need to make a new understanding with your insecure self, accepting that you are not a superhero but can do at least one little heroic deed every day.

In short, do not allow these parts of your mind to always win (and on all fronts)—drag them to the negotiating table and impose your new terms. As we have seen (and as it happens in every self-respecting negotiation), at some point, you will necessarily have to give ground and give it to laziness, fear, or insecurity, but decide right now that you do not intend to retreat even an inch. At the negotiation table, you must be in charge and in control. At the end of the day, shifting the burden or decision to have uninformed biases or insecurities, will leave you vulnerable and weak. As with negotiation, sometimes you compromise, and other times you enforce your will. Being the master of your game is necessary if you intend to make headway with the decisions you have brimming in your mind.

Break the best of deals with yourself and bring home the results you've always deserved. Your results will depend on how successful you have been in making your terms and conditions the main part of the bargain. Since the bargaining power is with you and yours, you can be sure to deliver your bundle of opinions and expect them to be at the core of the decisions.

ORWELL WAS WRONG

"Old Orwell was wrong. Big Brother doesn't watch us. Big Brother sings and dances. He constantly pulls rabbits out of his hat. 'Big Brother' is busy keeping your attention every moment of your day. He makes sure you're always distracted, makes sure your attention is fully absorbed, and makes sure your imagination dies slowly until it's as useful as your appendix. Make sure your attention is always busy. Being constantly distracted is far worse than being. Watch yourself. If they're in control of your attention, they don't need to worry about what you're thinking. If we all end up with our imaginations atrophied, no one will ever be a danger to the system." Chuck Palahniuk.

Today, more than ever, under the constant bombardment of weapons of mass distraction, protecting our attention is vital. If this week you find yourself in the trap of "Big Brother" (social, YouTube, TV & co.), Think back to the words of Palahniuk and choose to rebel. This need to rebel is necessitated by the hardships created by the very design of the system we have found ourselves in. The kind of system we have been raised in is one that is replete with distractions of many kinds that do nothing but drive us into wanderlust; even as we negotiate various paths further and get lost, our attention and focus are placed on things of little or no significance. We dwell in an age of binge information where the information doing the rounds is anything but barely sprinkled with truth.

Rebel against a system that doesn't give a damn about your goals and is willing to manipulate you to pursue its own interests, exploiting all your subtlest psychological vulnerabilities. If you are within a system that does not allow you to thrive but puts you constantly in a survival mode, you must reject such an order and stick with that which endorses and fuels your growth and development comprehensively. You cannot allow the system to mess with your mind and crash the ceiling of your mental and psychological strength. Even if the system seems built against you, like you are swimming against the tide, it is high time you made your choices.

Rebel against this dictatorship of distraction that floods us daily with futile information, depriving us of the opportunity to acquire real knowledge. True knowledge seems very scarce in this age with the doubling and tripling of data and information on an almost hourly, if not minutely, basis. With information abundance comes a lot of untruths and some half-truths, which do more harm than good and tend to cause friction among members of society. With the aid of the media, false information spreads like wildfire, and it becomes very difficult to distinguish between black, white, and grey. Distractions are also on the sidelines, seeking to lure our attention away from the more salient matters. For example, the luster, glitz, and glamour of entertainment and showbiz shine brighter at us, diverting our attention away from matters that require our attention. We have information abundantly, but we are not necessarily equipped with the right information to help navigate our path better. Then, it is up to us to be the difference and guard our attention diligently while also making sure to direct our attention to the other matters of importance.

Rebel against your procrastination and choose to use your attention to realize your most ambitious dreams, not those of some Silicon Valley tycoon. You must choose to make the essential moves and quit sulking or being bedridden with the I-will-do-it-tomorrow syndrome. The backlog of events that procrastination causes are enough to cripple your whole enthusiasm when you later find the strength to change the narrative. Rebel now against that procrastination and the vain glories you may have witnessed.

The choice is yours to rebel. No one can do it better than you.

THE LUXURY

In a recent interview, to the question "What is your idea of luxury?" Brunello Cucinelli, considered the king of cashmere, as well as one of the most enlightened Italian entrepreneurs, gave a beautiful answer, in my opinion:

"True luxury is living a life that is secret to your smartphone. Who does not have to know if I am going for a walk in the woods or if I am in Camogli to speak at a conference? This is the luxury that elevates the human soul and brings it closer to great beauty."

In this digital age rife with various social media platforms and avenues to seek validation, many people have lost total control over how they live their lives. They live their lives based on social media algorithms and the likes and followers available on various platforms. It is becoming increasingly difficult for some to detach themselves from the assent that the general social media populace tends to give to those who wear the trending luxurious items or are doing the big business stuff. For some, their smartphone becomes the center of their universe, a luxury in which they can only find solace. As the days roll by with new apps and sites being reeled out and new gadgets being introduced into the industry, many people have suddenly lost control over their schedules and how they live their lives. Their lives have become ruled under the government of their devices, and they are under what should be described as a form of "validation mania," where social media is seen as the validator of opinions and decisions in one's life. This poor sense of living has derailed some from the original purpose they possessed the luxury for, and they have become possessed by the spirit of the luxury to the extent that their desires become inordinate and spiral out of control.

The true beauty of life is to become both a possessor and a controller of that which you own. Whatever luxury you have, you must be the one in charge, and you must live your life outside of its purview. One thing with luxury is that it comes with a sense of fulfillment and pride that keeps us craving more to expand our ownership of luxurious products. We always want to own the latest and trending matters, events, and property. This comes at a price that we may not be so willing to pay. As with benefits, we must also reconcile with the fact that there are likely vices that may arise out of their abuse or misuse. These things must be anticipated and curbed while they can be.

Luxury is no validator of wealth or satisfaction. While it is good to purchase luxury items, there must be a guide that keeps that habit in check. We must not allow ourselves to be led off the precipice and fall headlong into the ditch unsuspectingly. In an era in which digital technologies have become increasingly invasive, the real luxury is, therefore, no longer owning the latest smartphone model but avoiding being owned by it. Being in control gives us leverage and security from mishandling. Hence, we are driven by the greater force of the good and harness these luxuries for our beneficial use. Like a horse, we can bridle our luxuries and rein in their excesses, but we can also guide them to the best usage possible.

THE 10 PERCENT TRAP

The other day I was reviewing some research on happiness that has always fascinated me. Researcher Sonia Lyubomirsky and her team from the University of California tried to answer a "simple" question: "What is it that makes us happy?" Or rather, what are the factors that impact our happiness?"

From the studies conducted, it emerged that, indeed, do you know what I tell you? First, I'll turn the question to you: what do you think are the ingredients of happiness? Health? Money? Social status? Mental attitude? Love?

If you had to bet a cup, which "horse" would you bet on?

Have you thought about your answer? Well, from Lyubomirsky's research (later confirmed by many other studies), it emerged that our happiness depends on 50% of our genes. So, watch out for the parents you choose! The role of the genes we get from our parents cannot be underestimated. Is this to say that we should be picky about our partners for the sake of our unborn children as well? Perhaps this will make us reconsider our choices.

We are also informed that 10% is from external factors (money, social status, physical appearance, etc.). Yes, of course, a particularly positive or negative event leads to a significant variation in our levels of happiness, but these then return to their previous values in a short time. A small fraction of our happiness is determined by some external factors that add value to our lives. When we have the wealth and wherewithal to attain our desires and attract what we will, there is a sense of gratification and happiness that accompanies us. Similarly, taking on an eminent position in society or socializing with high-ranking men and women in society may add some happiness to our work.

Finally, the remaining 40% depends on us, or rather on our inner dialogue, our mental attitude, and our habits. Did you read that right? Yet I bet that, a few minutes ago, when I asked you to think about the answer, you focused on that 10% that you focused on. Did I get it right? You might have thought that adding another artifact to your cache, a ride to your garage, or some huge funds to your bank account would endow you with the joy needed. You might even have thought that perhaps being able to sit at round conference tables and discuss political jargon or industry ideas with magnates and some top executives would do more than alleviate the sorrow you might be facing in your current state. Now, you see that almost half, apart from our genes, affect our rate of happiness and not what you were thinking earlier.

Do not worry; almost everyone falls into the "10% trap," believing that our happiness is out there and hanging from this or that event. And do you want to know what the real paradox is? If we work well on that 40% of factors under our control, we can create the fertile ground to condition even that 10% of exogenous factors in a virtuous circle in which happiness calls for new happiness. In other words, if we can work carefully on our mindset, habits, and actions, which, as repeatedly affirmed by top business executives and industry bigwigs, are the springboard for their excellence, we can orchestrate a magnetic system that attracts the rest of the 10% to us.

But this is where the $ 1 million question comes in: "How the hell can we act on our inner dialogue, our mental attitude, and our habits to be happier?" The truth of the matter is that happiness initially may not be visible. Discipline is not always a delightful experience, and finding happiness in it may seem like vain talk, but if we can weigh our chances, we'd know that we are on the right course and that eventually, we'd be happier for it.

THE IRON COWBOY

A couple of years ago, I read the story of this madman who had decided to complete 50 Ironmans in 50 consecutive days in 50 different US states (the so-called 50-50-50 challenge). An Ironman is a particular type of extreme race that involves the completion, in a single session, of 3.86 km of swimming, 180.260 km of cycling, and 42.195 km of running. "No walk of health in short!"

The madman in question is James Lawrence, a Canadian-born triathlete nick-named The Iron Cowboy. Honestly, I had forgotten about this story until, a few weeks ago, I happened to see a documentary dedicated to the 50-50-50 company.

In the feature film entitled "*Iron Cowboy*," in fact, James is followed for the duration of his challenge. Seeing him grind km after km, swimming, cycling, and running for 12-13 hours a day and then moving in a caravan along the American expanses to reach the next state in which to compete, sleeping just 2-3 hours a night, has some 'unbelievable. It really makes you think about what the real potential of the human body is, yet what struck me, particularly about this documentary, was the moment James was there to give up (roughly after the 30th consecutive Ironman).

One thinks that it will be due to the enormous physical and mental fatigue he has experienced during the journey.

It will be due to the crash on the bike a few days earlier and that that singular act would have been enough to make him reject doing another again, or that it will be due to the disorganization of the support team.

No, it is none of these at all.

The Iron Cowboy, the man who until then managed to complete 30 cal of Iron-man in a month, in 30 different states, in the most absurd weather conditions, is about to give up because of the negative comments that the company was receiving at that time on social media. This poor Christ was making a challenge to the limits of what is humanly possible and, punctually, every day was flooded with digital manure by people sitting on the sofa who had to object to the timely compliance with paragraph 24.B of section 3 of the Salamanca Regulation!

However, this background made me reflect on two things:

1) No matter what you do in life, someone will have something to say about it; it could be your parents, friends, colleagues, or a complete stranger sitting on an armchair behind a keyboard while you are sweating your 180 km of the day! You can never be short of critics at the end of the day. All of your actions and inactions will be scrutinized and either applauded or condemned by those around you. The likely problem you will encounter is that you might not know who will say what. Critiques are part of the culture, and one is not bereft of them unless one chooses to distance oneself from the community.

2) You may be the worst triathlete in the world and have developed superhuman physical and mental stamina, but if you don't learn to shield your thoughts from the judgment of others and your own negativity, you are screwed. This is the major point that sums it all up. One of the things you must learn as you advance in life and your career is to develop defenses to shield your mind from the naysaying of people. Not developing a thick skin that is tough enough to repel negative speech and mindset will turn out to be part of the greatest wrongdoing to be committed. In one singular stroke, another person can ruin your years of building, leaving you with nothing more than the restart button so you can begin all over again. Shielding your thoughts may include acting actively, like toughening up or beefing up your mental security, or acting passively, by avoiding negative comments that do nothing but pierce your soul evilly. It is okay to maintain a

distance from people who make you doubt your dreams and goals.

You must make sure you protect your mind and heart jealously. Let no one discourage you.

THE 25 THINGS WE HAVE FULL CONTROL OVER

In a world that goes faster and faster and is traversed by growing political, economic, social, and ecological restlessness, the risk of feeling at the mercy of events is very strong.

However, we must remember that, even in the greatest storm, there is always our sphere of control, that is, the set of decisions and actions over which we have full control.

Here are 25:

1. **The commitment you put into it.** The sum of the energy we put into life acting out our parts and the fervent of our relationships with people is one thing we have power over. We can choose to be committed or not, or even the varying levels of commitment that we want to have towards people, work, our family and friends, academics, relationships, etc. You can choose how committed you want to be to such things as even your personal growth.
2. **Your attitude.** Your behavior is your choice; you can choose to act and react however you want to. Even under tense conditions, you may

decide to avoid an outburst and keep your calm until the storm blows over. No one has a better grip on your attitude than you yourself. You have complete control over how you interact with others. It is dutiful to shape one's attitude, regardless.

3. **The way you react to your thoughts.** When you think something up, you can choose to act on it or not. Some are slaves to their thoughts and seldom do anything but what they think they should do.

4. **The actions you perform.** What you do is something that you have control over. It is often said that actions speak louder than words. So, it's your decision at the end of the day to choose to act in one way or another you can also decide to shun acting in a particular way as well.

5. **Your integrity**: You have control over your integrity, the veracity of your words, and the bulk of your virtues as a person. It is entirely up to you whether you choose to follow virtues or vices. How you display your integrity also matters a lot. You have the ability to make commitments and fulfill them. This will solidify your integrity.

6. The kindness you show.

7. The education with which you behave.

8. **The words you speak.** You can choose to control your tongue during moments of happiness, anger, sadness, or disappointment. You do not want to use your tongue to inflict any form of injury on others. It's very important that you choose the words you speak carefully and don't say what you do not mean or what you do not intend to do. Sensitive moments can bear a burden on one, forcing one to be vituperative, callous with words, or too loose with words. Bridling one's tongue is important here.

9. The words you write.

10. **What you eat and drink.** You must have control over your diet. Food that will put you at risk of diabetes, heart disease, and other diseases

should be avoided. You can train your appetite to be in consonance with health standards.

11. The products you buy.
12. The books you read
13. **The TV shows you watch.** You should be cautious about how much and what kind of shows you watch. Anyone that is offensive, misleading, offensive, or unethical should be avoided.
14. **The profiles and social pages you follow.** The contents of the people you follow will be reflected in your actions and daily life.
15. Your level of training.
16. Bad habits that you don't give up.
17. The good habits you choose to establish.
18. The friends you choose.
19. The kind of friend you choose to be.
20. The love you give.
21. The order in which you keep your space
22. With the money you spend.
23. The money you save.
24. The money you invest in.
25. The time you waste

HARU THE CARPENTER

There was once a carpenter named Haru, known throughout Tokyo for the quality of his buildings. His work was particularly appreciated by nobles, wealthy traders, and other notables of the city due to his relentless pursuit of excellence and his continued willingness to learn new techniques, even in the latter part of his career. Haru had worked hard for years, but he was starting to feel tired and wanted to stop working.

For more than 30 years, he had built the most beautiful houses in all of Tokyo, and now his dream was to travel and spend time with his grandchildren. Haru talked about it with his boss, who was grateful to the carpenter but made a final request:

"Dear Haru, our company will always be in debt for your magnificent work. We would like to ask you one last favor, however. Building one last house? It is a fundamental project for one of our most important customers. Here in the company, we all agree: we need your magic touch!"

Haru was very frustrated by the request; he would have to cancel a long-booked trip and postpone the start of his new life. He, therefore, asked his boss to give him a day to reflect. After discussing it with his wife, albeit reluctantly, Haru decided to accept the job. In all his work, the carpenter had always been very diligent and carefully chose the best materials, ensuring that every detail of the construction was perfect. But not for this house.

The idea of completing this project weighed too much on him, which is why he had delegated many of the activities, which impacted the final quality of the construction. Of course, the house met all legal requirements, but it was far from being one of the many masterpieces with which Haru had amazed the city over the years. Deep in his heart, the carpenter knew he had not worked up to his standards, but his head was now elsewhere.

When the work was done, Haru went to his boss and said: "The house is finished, as you requested. My wish now is to finally be able to retire." To which his boss said, "Thank you, Haru, thank you very much! We only have one last request for you."

The carpenter's frustration and anger grew further at those words, but the manager pulled a small package with a red bow from a drawer of his desk and handed it to Haru.

"We are very grateful to you for your work over the past 30 years, Haru. This gift is the way to show it to you."

Haru opened the package and found a set of keys inside. The chief smiled and said, "The house you built is yours!"

The carpenter's heart stopped for a moment. Without realizing it, Haru was building his house all this time. If only he had guessed, he would have taken care of every little detail with much more attention, but by now, it was too late.

This story teaches us two things:

First and foremost, Haru's boss is a great son of a bitch (joking...).

The second point is that we work on our "house" every day and often don't realize it. We study half-heartedly, more to meet exam deadlines than to increase our preparation. We work without particular enthusiasm, more for the salary at the end of the month than to excel in our career. We train absent-mindedly, more out of duty than out of a real desire to heal our temple (our body). We are too focused on the end result, and we fail to recognize that only by honoring the daily process, only by putting body and soul into every action, can we transform ourselves into the person deserving of realizing the dreams we have always imagined.

Face every action with the knowledge that you are building your "home" and building yourself. And remember, "The way you do the little things determines how you do all the things."

WINGS OF WASPS

For some time now, the climate has been particularly hot. A scorching heat such as this has not been seen for years. The other day I was in the garden to take care of the vegetable plants, but, unlike usual, I didn't do it in the early hours of the morning. But I had to take care of the plants just before noon, in the terrible heat. After placing the tools near a large vase, I suddenly saw myself surrounded by a swarm of wasps; they must have been 50 in number or thereabout, and no, I'm not kidding. Suddenly, I walked away from the scene. But then, I didn't have time to walk so far before one of them got to me, and one of them got to prick me in the arm. Initially, the sting from the wasp was a bit bad, but then I went back into the house, put ice in it, and luckily everything passed in a few minutes. It was surprising that something that had previously hurt so badly was just going to pass away like nothing in a few minutes.

It had never happened to me before that I was stung by wasps in that part of the garden, despite spending so much time in it. I go there every day. Since I usually go to the garden early in the morning, I simply had never seen them. They have always been there, but only in the heat do they become active and ready to sting. Then I reflected on the fact that, in reality, the most dangerous part of a wasp is not the sting but the wings. A wasp with a super sting full of poison, but without wings, could never have chased me in the garden, let alone sting me. But a wasp with wings is capable of doing that.

Without the ability to use the weapon he possesses, even the most fearsome of wasps would, in fact, be harmless, regardless of the weapon's power. So I, though stung by the sting, was actually defeated by the wings, not the sting, not the poison.

This has taught me to carefully evaluate every threat, every challenge, and every competitor. It is easy to make mistakes in evaluations, allowing oneself to be distracted by something flashy and threatening when the source of the difficulties is much deeper. It is useless to evaluate a difficulty without investigating its causes. System factors are much more important than the circumstances they create. So you must not fail to ask yourself questions from time to time, like: Are you evaluating your problems well? Do you dwell on the difficulties, or do you also evaluate the causes? Are you afraid of the sting, or do you realize that what will really hurt you are the wings?

THE DEFINITION OF SUCCESS

What was the first mental picture you had when you read the word "success?" My suspicion is that some people take it for granted that there is a single definition of success imposed by society and in which, rightly, not all are reflected. I am personally convinced that one of the first steps in one's personal growth path must be precisely that of identifying one's own personal idea of success. That's why I thought I'd share my favorite definition of success with you today. I hope it inspires you to find yours.

Laugh often with your family, friends, and loved ones. People get so much of this that they often fail to underestimate its power. But the truth is that success is not only restricted to how much you can acquire in life or how many degrees you are able to bag. But beyond this, those little moments we spend with our family, friends, and loved ones must not be downplayed at all. Always remember that the little things actually matter as well. Gain the respect of intelligent people and the affection of children.

The truth remains that your self-worth, though it has a lot to do with your own perspective on yourself, cannot merely be restricted to that narrative alone. Hence, you should not displace the space of being of value in the presence of people as well. And in this case, not just anyone, but the people that really matter. Listen to the praise of sincere critics and endure the betrayal of false friends.

In life, we are all going to experience awkward moments when those who are closest to us turn out to be the ones that can do that one thing that damages us and jeopardizes a lot of things about us, but in these moments, we must learn not to define ourselves by experiences like this but to keep on pressing towards the mark until we ensure that we arrive at that desired destination. Remember that not everything in this journey is won.

So, you lose some, and you win some. Appreciate beauty. People appreciate the beauty in people and in themselves as well, and always find a way of having beautiful things around them. Whether it is the beauty of nature or people in general, never despise them because therein lies a great dose of greatness as well. In addition to this, I also appreciate it when beautiful things happen to other people as well. In no time, you will find that beautiful things find their way to you too.

There are always good qualities in others. If you look closely within, you will discover that in everyone, there is a dosage of greatness that lies within. Acknowledge that, although they may not seem to look like it at the moment, there is something unique, something distinct, that can eventually spring out of everybody. Leaving the world a little better, be it a healed child, a flower bed, or redemption from a social condition, knowing that even one existence was happier because you existed. Here, this is to be successful. R.W. Emerson.

STARDUST

Sometimes, taken up by our occupations and worries, we forget who we really are. 13.8 billion years ago, the universe as we know it began with an explosion of unimaginable dimensions (the Big Bang). In a fraction of a second, the entire cosmic mass, concentrated in an infinitesimal point, began to expand. That "cosmic soup" has spread and cooled for millions of years, giving birth to celestial bodies. Among these, the stars are the space forges within which the fundamental chemical elements have been forged.

Those same elements of which every living being is made up. We ourselves are an unlikely combination of this "stardust." A combination so rare that it is aware of itself and the outside world. And this property, consciousness, despite having been studied for centuries by philosophers, men of faith, thinkers, and scientists, still remains today as one of the greatest mysteries of the universe.

Being aware of ourselves and the world around us is, in fact, at the same time, the most familiar experience—an experience that we relive every morning as soon as we wake up—but also the most enigmatic. In short, we humans are the universe that becomes aware of itself. Here, don't forget the next time you find yourself lost in some ephemeral bullshit. Look up!

Remember who and what you really are.

OBSESSION

Since every beautiful story begins with the words "once upon a time," then let me tell you one thing. Once upon a time, a 14-year-old boy asks a famous French chef, "Chef, what advice do you want to give to someone like me who wants to pursue this career?" The master then responded, "Be obsessive in what you are doing. Always stay by your professor's side, even if others tell you you're a lark. Learn."

Then, at one point, they knock on the door of a place nearby. Actually, it was the best restaurant in Paris and asked if there was an opening to be able to do something on your days off, even if it's polishing the dishes first. Then you will start washing them, then tasting something, and so on, weekend after weekend. As you work, you will start to earn some money: invest it in going to Lyon to see how a great chef cooks there and in Spain, Northern Europe, and Italy. But always remember that your roots are in your country. By doing so, you will learn that you have chosen a life of sacrifice and passion, the same one that will not make you feel the fatigue of work. Cooking will become part of your "self." Guess what the one word in the whole speech that some people have been focusing on? That's right; you guessed that "obsessive" is bad and ugly!

Well, the truth is that achieving excellence (in any area) requires a healthy dose of obsession. One of the effects of becoming obsessed is that it gives you the motivation to keep pursuing your desires and aspirations no matter how difficult things become. Of course, we must be careful so that healthy obsession does not become unhealthy because it is possible that, at times, obsession becomes quite unhealthy. That is, the ability to alternate moments of absolute dedication to moments of complete regeneration does not turn into a sick obsession, but it is precisely here that our good habits come to our aid: regenerating sleep morning routine; healthy diet; sporting activity; moderate use of social networks and smartphones.

It is, therefore, essential to feed our dreams. Knowing how to identify the best habits for our life and having an effective method to train them every time (while managing to abandon the bad ones) is essential to our success.

HARD TIMES

What we are currently experiencing in the world today are exceptional times. There are many events taking place around us that are very much capable of sweeping us off our feet. Some of these events are: the recent pandemic that caught the whole world unawares and destabilized the usual course of regular world order; the coronavirus, which manifested itself in more or less serious forms; the ever-increasing prices of goods that are necessary for our day-to-day survival; numerous wars taking place all around the world; cultural disintegration of society; the list could go on and on and on without an end; What is most confronting is the fact that, in the face of these events, the vast majority of us will be forced to radically change our habits, goals, and lifestyles (indeed, we have already started to do so).

Change, however, is something that not all of us find convenient to engage in. The process can be quite confronting at times and quite debilitating at others. The truth remains that, regardless of how challenging these times can be, there are still certain actions that we can take. These actions, though seemingly trivial to a far-reaching extent, have a grave impact on how well we can navigate through these hard times. Faced with these challenging situations, surreal until recently, we have several solutions, which are:

To stop hiding under the shadow of being fine so as not to be seen as a frail person. Occasionally, it is very okay to break down and let it all out. It is also very normal to cry at times in response to our plans going up in smoke.

To pretend as though all these things happening around us are non-existent and then continue living our regular day-to-day life in stubbornness, taking superficial advice from the experts and regulations in force either out of ignorance or for personal gain. Thus, we put ourselves and others in danger.

Utilize these moments as an avenue to embark on deep reflection. Here, you can live in the moment as an opportunity to deeply-reflect and review your life to improve on it radically. This story isn't just about personal growth; it can also be used to talk about the growth of a country.

The fact is that moments of difficulty like these are not merely designed to break us. If we pay keen attention to these moments, there are certain lessons that can be gleaned from them. Moments of distress, such as the one that the world is in currently, if utilized properly, can serve as an avenue to awaken us from numbness and also remind us that in life, even when things go far away from what we planned, it is still very possible to pick up what is available at our disposal and begin to leverage it to make the best out of every given opportunity. Moments like this remind us that we can always aspire to be the best version of ourselves, even if everything around us dictates otherwise and all odds seem to be against us. So, rather than being a victim of whatever the world throws at us, now is the perfect time to go above and beyond these difficult times to be not only reactive but also very proactive at all times. To a far-reaching extent, our disposition during these times will determine how well we turn out to be and how relevant we are in totality.

In the words of the renowned G. Michael Hopf, it can hence be concluded that:

Quiet times create weak men.

Weak men create bad times.

Adverse times create strong men.

Strong men create quiet times

My advice is, therefore, to live the many limits that this period is imposing on us to slow down, reflect, and finally find time for ourselves and our personal growth as well.

IGNORE THE REST

While there may be a lot of noise around us that wants to dictate how we should live our lives at such a time like this, we must ensure that we stand very strong against the tide and be what we want to be and not what we ought to be. There are certain things that we absolutely need to hold on to if we are going to make the best out of our lives. These are not actions that should be embarked on by a survivor. They are rather the actions of a conqueror. Hence, anyone who sincerely desires to maximize their existence must hold on to it vehemently. You are probably wondering what it could be that wields so much power over the existence of a person who really wants to make the best out of their life. Well, see for yourself. The list below is captured in a tweet put forward by Naval Ravikant.

Defend your sleep. No man was designed to work all day. Just like the popular saying that says all work and no play makes Jack a dull boy. This truth, as well, applies even in the context of sleep. As well as we work, we must also not take away the place of sleep. What sleep does is that it helps us to revitalize ourselves and perform effectively in our subsequent engagements.

Train your strength—everyone has a strength. That innate ability that is embed ded within us is our strength. Usually, a person will always find it very convenient to partake in things that are their strength. They do it almost effortlessly. This doesn't, however, mean that we should be convenient where we are. Even if we tag it as our "strength," the truth remains that there is always room for improvement at all times. So, train your strength. Invest in it voraciously.

Train your heart: As we train our muscles, it is also very necessary that we do the same with our hearts. A disciplined heart can achieve, factually, anything. Though the process may be quite inconvenient, one thing you need to understand is that, in the end, it will always be worth it. Hence, do not despise the act of disciplining your heart. Ensure that your attention is not diverted from the end result you have in view at all times. This matters to you a lot.

Train your flexibility: If there is any lesson to be learned from life, it is that life is subject to change at any time. Hence, it is very important that as you progress in life, you train yourself to be very flexible to change and to its demands because, to a far-reaching extent, it will determine how well you can condition yourself to push further in the face of difficulties.

Meditate: It is also very important that you build a habit around the act of meditating regularly. Meditating helps you keep your vision in perspective. It also allows you to clear your mind off excess and irrelevant thoughts that may arise as you move through the hustle and bustle of life.

Be aware of what you eat.

Build something of value: One of the things that you absolutely need to invest in as you journey through life is that you build something of value. At the end of it all, this is the only way that it is possible to live a legacy and leave a legacy behind you. So, invest in people, places, and everything else that has value.

Writing, or as it is popularly known as journaling, offers immense value to anyone who engages in the act. There is a popular saying that the faintest pen is sharper than the sharpest brain. So, writing rids you of forgetfulness. It also helps you process your thoughts properly before executing them.

Save and invest, read, reflect, love, seek the truth, relax, avoid debts, avoid addictions, and avoid the news as much as possible. Focus on these actions and make them habits. Ignore everything else; they do not matter as much.

THE ANTI-GOALS

Something that is largely scarce in our world today is the fact that there are two ways to achieve any goal that a person wishes to achieve. One is to approach the goal by having it directly in view, and the other is to avoid doing the opposite of what you want to achieve. Although these two ways work, it turns out that the latter is always more effective than the former. Now let's give perspective to the discussion.

For instance, if you want to be a brilliant person, rather than directly aiming at it, you can still achieve it by avoiding being stupid. Hence, "instead of trying to be brilliant, simply avoid being stupid." The way to achieve it is very simple. You can easily translate this principle into practice by using anti-targets. When most people want to accomplish a certain goal, they start thinking about how they can add things to their life. So, we hear them say things like: maybe I should get up at dawn to get it done; maybe I should try that diet everyone is talking about; maybe I should download that meditation app; and so on.

The problem with adding new activities to that list and committing ourselves to new events is that they either don't work or experience a lot of difficulties in the execution process. A much more effective strategy to achieve goals is using the ANTI-GOALS strategy. In other words, rather than spending all your time thinking about what you can add to yourself, you can spend your time thinking about what you can subtract from yourself.

For example, if you want to be a more productive student or a more lucrative worker, before embarking on the things that you may consider to be most important, like having a sophisticated time management system, you can proceed by asking yourself what negative habits are taking your time and withholding you from achieving the things that you want to. Then proceed to put a stop to them. Yes, it is always that simple because we often find ourselves struggling to become flexible to new developments that we frequently neglect the filtering of the old things that have become a burden and have no positive result in our lives, and this is where the effectiveness of the anti-goal strategy comes into play.

Do you want to get in shape again? Even before starting that Hollywood star training program, ask yourself how you can reduce all those hours you spend sitting. Do you want to boost your earnings? Even before adding new products, new services, and new customers, ask yourself what business bottlenecks are costing you time and money and how you can eliminate them.

Having said that, in your life, you must grow in the understanding that you won't always be able to give yourself anti-goals, but asking yourself what you can stop doing is often the most immediate way to start getting concrete results. So, while everything that you are engaged in may not be able to function under the anti-goal strategy, you can begin your journey by asking simple questions. Take a moment, reflect on your life, and find out those things that seem not to yield results in the way you desire. Once you identify them, then you will know what to do next. So, what's stopping you from utilizing the anti-goal strategy? Now is the perfect time to start.

THE NEW BEGINNING

Symbolic dates are always full of good intentions. This is basically because they often come with a lot of planning, resolutions, and the like. There is this nudging within us that is often associated with symbolic dates. We want a new beginning, something very different, if not completely different, from what it used to be for us. Well, everyone goes around with such feelings, and you are probably not an exception in this regard. Moments like this can surface at any time that we somehow feel connected or attached to. So for some, it could be the first day of the year, their birthday, a special date, or it could literally be any time that is special to them. Moments like these are often good for planning a zero point from which to start something new. Those who think so are intimately convinced that starting from the infamous symbolic date will finally give them a clean break from the past! So, here are a few things you can do to ensure your plan to start over at a certain time doesn't fall through.

Stop procrastination. Procrastination never helps you out in any way. It just prevents you from being able to achieve things that you want to. If you have a plan, then now is the best time to begin to execute it. A stitch in time saves nine.

No more laziness. If there's anything those new seasons do to you, it is that they inject you with the urge and the zeal to act upon your desires and resolutions. So, since zeal and passion are available, then the last thing you need to do is hold on to laziness. Act on your desires, be hardworking, and you'll realize progress in a short time.

Enough cigarettes; there is no positive effect that cigarettes offer that is permanent. Hence, it can appease you for a while, but rest assured that it will have debilitating repercussions if you proceed with the act. Cigarettes only offer temporary pleasure. In the long run, it has more negative effects than positive ones.

No more sweets. Sweets can be quite addictive. You feast on them for a while and get so used to it that you find quitting very difficult. But the truth is that it may actually be doing you harm health-wise. So you must stop feasting on sweets as much as possible.

From that day on, you will discover that somehow everything just turns out to be perfect. Yes, everything will finally be perfect. So, as you launch into a new phase in a new season, you should create a habit around meditating, preferably at dawn. You could take an hour to meditate, shirtless, under a cascade of frozen water. You should also run off to complete your daily half-marathon while listening to a quantum physics audiobook. Once you arrive for breakfast, you should eat a perfect Keto-Paleo-Vegan-Blood group meal. Before lunch, you should have already completed a thousand micro-intervals of work under the careful supervision of the saint of Prof. Cal Newport, patron of Deep Work.

Starting from the fateful date, you begin to embark on this journey, and then you realize that everything will finally be different. You will finally be different. Or, to put it another way, WE will finally be different. Yes, because we all struggle to initiate something, some more than others. Despite numerous failed attempts to demonstrate otherwise, we believe that a date to which society arbitrarily assigned a different meaning is the key to our turning point. And so, we regularly find ourselves falling into the trap of new and perfect beginnings. The truth is that each of us had only one real beginning (and that took 9 months of gestation!).

Since then, we have been playing the same imperfect game called life.

Sometimes, we are ahead, and sometimes, we are behind.

Sometimes, we run like trains, and in others, we have to catch our breath.

The wish I want to make you is to free you from the illusion of perfect new beginnings.

Do not work. They never work.

Accept where you are and what you are doing right now.

Accept that you will continue to have imperfect days.

Accept the inevitable failures and setbacks.

Accept your perfidious, indisputable, unknowable imperfection. May this acceptance be your real new beginning.

TOUCH THE BOTTOM

What comes to your mind when you hear those three words "touch the bottom?" Well, do not go about thinking too far. You are just about to find out what it means. Let me tell you the story of a particular person who goes by the name "the bottom touched." That was his name in full, but he was often addressed as BT. BT is just a regular classic person who first feels the need to touch the bottom to find motivation. In other words, it was his custom to hit rock bottom before becoming motivated to act.

So, what he does is quite simple yet confounding. He spends many hours focusing on things that would ordinarily not be advantageous to him. So, BT watches several movies on Netflix for several hours. He could go as far as spending up to 12 hours on Netflix; the more movies he saw, the more he wanted to watch. For him, he never seemed to get enough of these movies in a way that suited his yearning. So there is always an innate craving for more.

Besides this, BT also spends the other 12 hours watching idiotic reels on Instagram before feeling so remorseful that he has done a scant half hour of study or focused work. That sounds ridiculous, right? But yes, that was BT for you. The one person who always had to wait until all the time was completely exhausted before he embarked on something meaningful. BT leaves the groove of his buttocks well imprinted on the sofa and waits for the scale to read "red alert" before deciding to make a minimum of physical movement. He was that comfortable with being irrelevant. As long as it didn't call for panic, he was perfectly alright. BT also buys the 2000 turbo-version incline bench with a free abdominal tool and waits for the bank to call it, warning it of the Amex block, before committing to getting its finances back on track.

In short, BT is nothing short of an Olympic champion of self-sabotage and self-harm. So, the only thing that brings chaos to BT is no one other than himself. As if that weren't enough, he often finds himself stuck in this vicious circle in which the famous "bottom" is lowered more and more, and the thrust he manages to get back up every time he touches it is becoming increasingly weak.

Well, maybe you are a "BT" at a beginner level, but if you have come to read this far, some of my words have likely made deep chords resonate in you. Because BT is, in fact, not so far from you, it may sting you to know, but you just may be BT. Always wait till the last minute before deciding to get actively involved in the things that actually require more attention from you. Well, the good thing for you to know is that being a BT is not a process that doesn't have an end in itself. So the problem is not about whether or not you are a BT, but rather whether you want to remain one or to break the shackles and be something more. This then brings us to the question, "How can we get out of the frustrating jumbo of being a BT then? How can we stop self-sabotaging and finally regain motivation in a healthy way?"

Well, the answer is not complex. It lies in secret, and the secret in these cases is to kill our "monsters" while they are still little ones. It is much easier to overcome bad habits while they are still being formed in us rather than waiting until they become a full-fledged challenge before we address them, which is the mistake that most people make. They wait for such a long period before taking their monsters down until they subsequently discover that they have become their own monsters and are a stumbling block to themselves.

Did you miss a workout after a perfect sequence? Start again today; don't wait for perfect conditions to return. Do not waste any time thinking about it. Pick up your pieces and start right away.

Did you have the fight of the century with your partner? Try to talk to people as soon as possible; don't wait for the relationship to deteriorate further.

Have you been studying with the concentration of a sloth in the last few days? Do half an hour of super-focused study right away; don't wait for the start of a new hour, lunch break, or some other "magical" condition.

If you don't want the BT syndrome to ruin your life, you definitely have to learn how to get up after each fall, but above all, you have to learn how to do it as soon as possible.

Yes, I know; getting up sucks. Your muscles are still sore from the "fall," you are dirty with mud, and, as disheartening as it is, lying down after the effort you had made up to that point, in the end, is not so bad. If you don't get up right away, however, doing it later will become increasingly difficult, and there will come a day when you simply no longer believe you are capable of it. As you get up, you push the bottom at a distance equal to your height. It's not much, but it's better than nothing.

Get up even if you don't feel motivated.

Get up even if the conditions aren't right.

Get up even if you are afraid of relapsing. Just make sure you get up!

...And finally, get up today!

TIME MANAGEMENT

When it comes to time management, many readers immediately think of complicated systems made up of calendars, agendas, to-do lists, and so on. In reality, the idea of time management is not restricted to the aforesaid alone. Beforehand, there are some basic principles that must be understood first of all.

A principle that we could consider "trivial" but that almost none of us are able to apply consistently in our lives is the most important activity first. We could continue to stress it on social media, and we may even subconsciously believe

that it is our current reality, but it is not when we think about it carefully. If you have your smartphone in your hand right now, you probably haven't applied this principle today either.

There is little doubt that this principle of time management works.

Dedicating the early hours of the morning to our most important projects is also a way to ensure constant progress. The progress may not be dramatic because it was not intended to be, but its consistency ensures that it will produce results gradually and steadily.

Every day is full of unexpected events, and scheduling key activities in the afternoon or evening often means condemning them to "never." In short, in theory, we know very well that dedicating the first hours of study or work to our priorities is the correct way to proceed. In practice, however, we find ourselves checking emails every morning, reading the news to be aware of the latest happenings around us, checking social media for updates, and responding to urgent emergencies. We engage ourselves in every other activity. That is, except the ones that we ought to, which are the most important ones.

The next question to be asked is: why is it always so? Well, the answer largely depends on the social conditioning we have suffered for years. At school, we were taught to complete the imposed homework by teachers and professors. At work, they taught us to pay attention to any tantrums from our superiors. At home, they taught us to respect the requests of parents, relatives, and relatives. When an animal or even a human being is conditioned for years to react to external stimuli, she will hardly stop and listen to her true internal priorities. What I am introducing to you is not something that you do not already know. However, I am striking the consciousness in you once again for the sake of emphasis to redraw your attention to it. I am inviting you to become aware of these automatisms and to dedicate to your hopes, your dreams, and your projects the space they deserve. These things may not be as difficult to achieve as they seem if you get your priorities right in the correct proportion. Yes, that's one of the things that you need to tightly hold on to. You must not ignore your responsibilities as a citizen, professional, or family member.

Simply apply this fundamental principle of personal effectiveness for seven days. Simply carry out the activities that matter to you as the first thing every day and then watch to see what happens next. It'd be quite surprising that all you needed has been at your fingertips all along. You just need an accurate perspective on things and then a proper execution of your scale of preference. And by scale of preference, I do not merely talk about your desire. But I also talk about the things that really matter.

START OVER

The truth is, every one of us likes new beginnings. We all appreciate the feeling of having the opportunity to start something afresh. Yes, indeed, we may not all be afforded the opportunity to have to restart something. But then, even if it is a new habit, or developing a new skill, or anything in that vein, there is just this comforting feeling that accompanies starting afresh. We all cannot desire to trade the experience of a new beginning in whatever we are doing for something else. And yes, everyone feels this way. It is not just restricted to a set of people. I remember, while we were much younger, it was always an amazing experience to know that we would move into a new class. Yes, many of us knew that there were perhaps going to be just a few new faces around us, and not much was going to change, but anyway, the nerve fact that we were leaving something behind and then starting something entirely different was just so comforting. This case is what we all feel like when we get to experience a new beginning.

Each new beginning gives us the illusion that everything will finally be perfect, free from mistakes and falls. It gives us the opportunity to be the artists of our own lives and then to determine things the way we want them to be. So it is more or less like we are ignoring the past and holding on to the new. This is something that all of us want, right?

New beginnings are, in short, motivating and make us believe that our life has reached the fateful turning point we require at some point. But, moving on, we discover that, regardless of how intense the euphoria is, it rarely leads to true change because, in reality, it is the actions that should accompany the euphoria that affirms true change. Real change, in fact, depends on the ability to start over. So, while everything may seem like it is crumbling or going contrary to plan, it may be a perfect time to take a break, look behind you, and just begin everything or something all over again. One of the most amazing things about new beginnings is that it is never too late to start over, except if you consider it too late. So, if you do not think it is too late, then it is never too late to start over. Starting over after a bad day, starting over after a fall, starting over after a defeat, starting over after a mistake, starting over after a disappointment, starting over after a loss. Whatever the case may seem to have caused a setback in one way or the other, you should know that it is never too late to start it all over from the beginning and that now is the perfect time to start over.

Put aside the search for the perfect start and simply start over with whatever you have at your disposal, accepting your mistakes and flaws as you proceed to a new beginning. You don't become unstoppable when you never fall, but when you rise again with each fall. It is the only one who falls that has any hope of rising again. So cheers to falling and rising again, and then cheers to new beginnings!

THE TEN HABITS

Over the years, I have thought about what the ten habits could be that we should never give up on to be masters of our lives. And I have finally come up with the appropriate list that best suits that description. Here's a walk-through of what I found out:

Go to sleep around 10 pm and wake up naturally (if you can). Sometimes it will be 5:00 in the morning, other times 6:00, and maybe, after a particularly intense workout, even 7:00!

Remember to be grateful for every little opportunity, but don't force yourself to keep a gratitude journal to fill out mechanically. Just say in the consciousness that you ought to be committed to always being grateful for life and every opportunity it brings.

Take five minutes to review the day's schedule and visualize your goals. Doing this gives you an edge at all times and reduces your risk of making mistakes.

Try to move daily, alternating strength, flexibility, and endurance workouts. Always ensure that you dedicate a period to being in motion.

Complete three important activities before 11 am. Yes, you should always make sure to finish three of your most important tasks before 11 a.m.

You should eat real, healthy, and varied foods at least six days a week. Enjoy free meals and experience intermittent fasting several times a month.

Take a picture of your finances once a month and pay for small daily expenses with cards linked to digital accounts that allow you to track them easily.

Describe your day in five lines. A diary is a very powerful tool for self-improvement. It makes you keep in touch with yourself, take notes of your progress, and hold on to that drive you need to keep your aspirations in perspective.

Dedicate at least an hour each day to yourself. Within this hour, you do not need to bother yourself with everything around you. Make this one hour of alone time solely for yourself. Time is the only egalitarian resource in the world. An hour is an hour for everyone, rich or poor, powerful or subordinate. Don't waste it. Use your time for yourself.

Read 30 minutes before falling asleep but feel free to ditch a book that isn't thrilling you even after 30 pages. Life is too short to read books that don't interest us.

This list is not made up of those "good and bad" people who like them so much on social networks, but it is certainly a list that most reflects my experience in recent years, and I hope it can give you some useful ideas too. Don't force yourself to follow them all or right away. Don't twist your life in the service of a list. The process through which you execute this list till you get accustomed to it must be gradual. It is in its slowness and steadiness that you can be sure you will succeed at it. And not just succeed, but succeed without having to go through the drastic process of building yourself around a specific habit.

Between miraculous routines and often too strict rules, most para-gurus forget that we are human beings, each with our own specific needs, and the approach that works for one person may not necessarily be effective if applied, utilizing the same methods to another person.

Simply pick the one that most impresses you from these ten habits to change your life and begin there. From there, you can gradually begin to take on the other ones till you find that you have already built a culture around these activities.

MODERATION AND HAPPINESS

The world of personal growth is ruled by excesses. Most of the time, when you come into contact with someone aspiring for growth in any sphere of his or her life, you often experience that the person is expected to live their life according to a specific manual. People often misinterpret the disciplined process that it takes to build something great as a ritual that requires certain condiments that must be present in the sacrifice. So you often hear things like:

-Wake up at 4:00

-Do yoga under a cold shower for 15

-Work or never get distracted.

-Delete your social accounts.

-Isolate yourself from the people around you if you perceive them as blockers.

-Run on hot coals

But the truth is far from it. Greatness requires discipline and sacrifice, but it does not necessarily need to follow a specific order. Some excesses often associated with greatness or the attainment of an individual's goals and aspirations make sense at certain moments in our lives. Yet, the more I progress on my personal growth path, the more I rediscover the value of the Aristotelian metrics (the right middle ground). Yes, I know, moderation is not a cool topic. In moderation, we prefer those beautiful extremes that deceive us into being able to radically change our lives, giving them a sharp turn! Only moderation can truly lead us to a profound and permanent change called happiness.

For the ancient Greeks, "happiness and unhappiness are phenomena of the soul, which feels pleasure or displeasure in existing depending on whether it feels or does not feel fulfilled" (Democritus). In other words, what this means is that happiness is mostly relative. It varies from individual to individual, and in this case, you can only be referred to as a happy individual once you have your definition or your idea of happiness met. So, it is very important that you precisely define your perspective on happiness.

Self-realization is, therefore, the deciding factor for happiness. But for self-realization, it is necessary to exercise that virtue capable of enjoying what is obtainable and not wanting what is unattainable. So the "right measure." The Greeks used to say, as a containment of desire, of the expansive force of life that, without measure, pushes men to want what is not in their power, thus declining their own "demon." Their inner disposition does not lie in happiness (eudaimonia) but in unhappiness (kako-daimonia), which is, therefore, the fruit of the misrule of oneself and one's own strength, clouded by the voluptuousness of desire.

So, not happiness as the fulfillment of wants or even happiness as a reward for being good, but virtue as the ability to control yourself for your own success.

In this sense, happiness is teachable. And in this sense, I decline my thought when I speak of "personal growth." Hence, in your journey to greatness, you must not just pursue what you want to achieve. Beyond that, you must ensure that you do things in moderation and also pursue them after moderation.

CHOOSE *'YOUR'* DIFFICULT

A constant thing about life is that difficulties are an integral part of it. They cannot be separated as everyone that walks the face of the Earth will, at one point or the other, be exposed to difficulties. To claim that you have escaped difficulty in life is to suggest that you have not even spent time living at all. It is possible that one moment you feel like you have everything all figured out, and then in the next moment, everything just comes crumbling.

This is not an unusual way for anyone who wishes to make a significant impact on the sands of time to feel. The truth is that everything in this world, at some point in time, turns out to be difficult. No matter how enticing and exciting the experience may be, it doesn't eliminate the fact that greatness is not bred overnight. It doesn't just take a long and difficult process to experience greatness, but the difficulty involved in maintaining greatness is even more confronting. It is safe to conclude from this that difficulties are an unavoidable part of life, both for those who are successful and those who are not.

Now, understanding that no one, regardless of their status, escapes difficulties, what should be the major subject of discussion is not how to maneuver through difficulties but rather how to select the right type of difficulty. So, getting married is difficult, getting divorced is difficult, being obese is difficult, and being fit is also not an exception as it requires great effort and attention. Debt is difficult, being financially free is difficult, being rich is difficult, maintaining good health is difficult, and keeping human relationships also requires so much effort and, as such, can also be tagged to be difficult. Think of anything you can. It is impossible to escape difficulty at each phase in life.

In short, life is never easy, whether we choose to commit ourselves to adopting good habits or if we find ourselves suffering the consequences of our bad habits. However, we can choose our difficulties, which is no small feat. It is a task that also requires attention because oftentimes, the things that we take pleasure in do not turn out to be what determines our greatness. So, we may be forced to take a leap out of our comfort zone and strive for something superior to our comfortability.

While you strive to ensure that your own choice of "difficult" is rightly positioned, one thing that you must never forget in the process is that, in the end, we will always pay the price; it is up to us to choose whether it will be the price of success or the price of regret. Now I bet no one wants to pay the price only to end up regretting it in the long run. As a result, as you go through the process of choosing your own challenge, keep in mind that you are not only making decisions for yourself but also charting the course for your ambition, aspirations, and, most importantly, your future. Hence, do not just choose your difficulties, but make sure you choose them wisely.

DISTRACTION

The world that we live in today is one that is interruption-focused. So, it's not surprising to come across someone who claims to be or has been distracted at some point in their lives. Most of the time, the littlest of all things and the tiniest of all details can get us distracted. Something as minor as a pop-up notification from our phone can literarily throw us into spending hours upon hours away from what we ought to actually be focused on.

Slowly, we begin to drift away from the things that should ordinarily be at the epicenter of our attention till we ultimately find out that we are far away from them entirely. Distraction can surface in several forms. There is that which takes place for a short period. And then there is the one that spans over a long period.

Whichever the case is, however, distractions can be very challenging at times, to such an extent that it throws a person into an utter state of confusion. This begs the question of how you can rise from the ashes, dust yourself off, and begin to take action to achieve whatever you desire.

Contrary to popular opinion, the opposite of distraction is not focus but traction. Sounds surprising, right? But that is the force that pushes us forward, pulls us, and attracts us towards a goal we really want. When we are distracted, it means that this attractive force is absent, and we find ourselves lost in a thousand directions, looking for some positive stimulus; some cheap dopamine injection. In these cases, brute discipline and willpower are not always the most effective answers to solving the problem. Far from it! Instead of hitting on us for being distracted, it's much more helpful to figure out how to rekindle our traction.

So, we need to find that force, that fossil fuel that will ignite our pursuit of the things we intend to achieve. What would really make our hearts beat right now, and is it aligned with our long-term values and goals? What naturally piques our interest? What draws us? What do we feel we want to create, build, or do at this very moment? Because these are the only things that can push us further whenever we get distracted from a specific goal we intend to achieve.

When we are distracted (and we are for too long), it is essential to find our center of gravity, the north of our magnetic pole. Reconnect with the purpose you started for the first time. There is a popular saying that the source is the cure. If you can intensely remember why you set out for your aspirations in the first place, it'd be easier for you to proceed with them. Also, if you find yourself in this situation right now, if, in this period, you tend to waste your time and energy on the thousands of tributaries of inconclusiveness, stop! Don't go around trying to force yourself into figuring everything out at once because if you do, it is most likely that confusion will set in. And confusion will do absolutely nothing more than giving room for unproductivity and clumsiness. So, if you find yourself in the snare of distraction, what you need to do is to stop. Put an end to the commotion. Stop pushing and listen carefully to where you are naturally attracted.

Find your traction once again, and you'll be back on track in no time.

THE BISON

The bison, when a storm arrives, starts running towards it. Now that sounds like a really crazy thing to do, doesn't it? But in truth, that is the way of people capable of standing firm against a turbulent tide. Doing so minimizes the time they spend feeling uncomfortable and wet. There is a common mistake that a lot of people make.

It is that when they merely perceive a difficult time ahead, they immediately take cover and shield themselves from colliding with it. We have many people phasing out when confronted with a difficult situation, which is why a larger population finds it impossible to manage difficult times and situations. One thing that people fail to understand is that, as it has already been said earlier in the course of this book, the storms (difficult times) were not designed to crush a person.

So, rather than take up the position of someone defined by difficult circumstances and situations, it's best to hit against the top and take up lessons that will serve as the roadmap for navigating the future properly. It is quite simple. In difficult times, do not make yourself driven by every wave of difficulty. Instead of that, stand firm against the storm, fall and pick up lessons as you rise again, and be prepared to face a whole new adventure in life. That's how it ought to be.

We human beings usually tend to postpone or avoid commitments, but these do nothing but accumulate in our heads, making us live in a perennial mental storm.

Be like a bison and run to meet the storm.

11 STEPS

I am reading a book that was recommended to me during this period. The title of the book is "*An impossible challenge*," and it was written by the American explorer Colin O'Brady and tells of his most famous feat to date: the solo crossing of Antarctica, without supplies and without the help of sails or sled dogs, carried out in 2018. Like the genre, it's a very nice book. At one point, O'Brady tells the tragic story of the Royal Navy officer Robert Falcon Scott, who lost his life with his men in 1912 on the way back from the South Pole. They starved to death. Their camp was found less than 20 kilometers from the food depot that would save them. Rescuers calculated that if the British explorer and his crew made an effort to take just eleven more steps at the end of each stop, then they would arrive safely at the refueling point. Of course, we do not have to cross hostile continents or reach vital food supplies in our daily lives. Yet those extra eleven steps can be a very powerful metaphor. How many times have we missed our goals by a hair's breadth? How many times have we given up a few "kilometers" from the goal?

Before you close the books on that exam you are preparing for.

Before you finish your workout.

Before concluding the activities of that personal project, make sure to take those eleven extra steps because maybe, just maybe, it is in them that the path to your success lies waiting for you.

Sometimes, the difference between failure and success lies in the small actions we choose to do or not do every day. I would like to share with you a very brief reflection, which I hope will inspire you.

Grapes must be crushed to make wine. The process may be quite unfavorable for the little grape, but it cannot be avoided. Hence, if a grape refuses to go through the strenuous process of being crushed, it may just never turn out to be wine. Similar to grapes, olives are also crushed to make oil. Diamonds are also created only under enormous pressure. Finally, seeds need darkness to grow. They need to be buried deep into the ground and then die before they have the hope of rising again and becoming something more beautiful, attractive, and fruitful.

So, if you are feeling crushed, broken, pressured, or in a dark moment in your life right now, remember that you are going through an important time of transformation. It's not the end; only if you choose to stand strong, resilient, and never give up will your success lie patiently ahead of you. So, do not give up; only trust the process.

You may just be this close to achieving that thing that you have always desired.

THE POWER OF EVERY HOUR

Achieving our most ambitious goals takes time, often far more than we initially imagined. Rome was not built in a day, they say. The same applies to your ambitions. You do not just walk into them as easily as you conceive them. No, it never works that way There will be hard times, regrets, discouragements, and what have you. All these are a process that, in reality, you cannot avoid. You must not neglect the power and possibility in the process. It could take months, if not years, before we finally see our dream come true. Within this period, a lot will probably have taken place, and every of it must not be despised because this all adds up to your success story in the future. This doesn't mean that what you do today is not important. Indeed, the opposite is true.

Every single day counts. Every single hour counts.

In the next 60 minutes, you can achieve literally anything that you wish to. You can complete the best-focused study/work session you've ever had in your life, begin that training program that you have been putting off for weeks and that will determine your well-being and health over the next 30 years, create a moment of connection and deep intimacy with your partner, read 30 pages of a book that has the potential to inspire you and revolutionize your life, take the first steps necessary to start that entrepreneurial activity thanks to which you will be able to achieve your goals, forgive in your heart that person who has held your serenity hostage for the past five years, improve the life of another person, helping him in a selfless way to solve a problem on which you have specific skills, make a solemn commitment to yourself to improve an area of your life. I am speaking of a real Roman Sacramentum, or the oath the ancient Latins made in front of their fellow citizens and gods, which could not be broken for anything in the world. In short, life is a marathon, but every single step counts. Do not despise the power of an hour. You think it is merely an hour until it passes by, then you realize that you have missed out on a lot of things.

Don't waste this week. Don't waste this day. Don't waste the next 60 minutes. They can just be the start of your new life.

"You can't go back and change the beginning, but you can start where you are and change the ending"—CS Lewis.

EXCESSES

Every excess covers a lack. So, anyone who chooses to spend so much time beyond the ordinary engaging in a specific activity is only trying to cover for a specific lapse. Whatever it is, a person is only utilizing the time they spend excessively on an activity to detox from the real issue that ought to be confronted. In this age of abundance, each of us has our own addiction.

There are those who spend too many hours on social media, there are those who eat too many sweets, there are those who get sucked into video games for too long, there are those who work long hours, there are those who spend an enormous amount of time studying, and there are those who consume so much food. The list can go on and on and on.

Even excluding pathological situations in which the intervention of a specialist is necessary, these "excesses" of ours can heavily affect our life. This is how, at the umpteenth "binge" of food, social media, or video games, we solemnly promise ourselves that that will be the last time, but time and again, we fall back and fail to meet our end of that commitment.

The fact is, trying to fight our excesses by willpower alone is a losing battle. It takes more than mere willpower to win a battle of excesses. The effective way is to identify what the lack (the need) is that we are trying to compensate for with that excess and take care of it in a conscious way.

When do you find yourself shaking your smartphone endlessly, eating whatever, or playing non-stop? Does it happen at a particular time of the day? Does it happen when you experience certain negative emotional states (tiredness, boredom, anxiety, sense of inadequacy, etc.)? Does it happen only in certain places or with certain people?

Find your trigger. Observe it without immediately giving in to your "addiction." Experiment with new, healthier ways to deal with that emptiness and sense of discomfort. Our excesses are there to remind us that there are areas of our lives that deserve our attention and that we can no longer bury our heads in the sand (or on our cell phone screens).

LUCK

There are three types of luck, and knowing them will help you become much luckier in your life.

1. You create your own luck. Lucky events, in fact, are nothing more than statistical anomalies. If we work hard enough on the right actions and for enough time, success will be inevitable. This further means that the fact that it is called "luck" doesn't make it a coincidence. Luck can be cooked up intentionally as well.
2. With luck that you find. You have probably heard less of the second form of luck. The luck you find is the luck that comes from skills and experience. When you become a true expert in a specific niche, industry, or profession, you develop the ability to spot trends and lucky events as they occur. And as a result, you are able to exploit them better than ordinary people. Increasing your skills in the areas you are passionate about will help you notice the right opportunities before others and find your luck.
3. Goodluck in locating you.

Effort and hard work will help you increase your chances of success. Skills and experience will help you spot lucky trends before they go mainstream, but only if you cultivate the uniqueness of your character and your personal brand will you be able to attract the most fortunate occasions to you.

Now, let me explain. At one time, there were few clear professional categories. Belonging to one of them guaranteed a good standard of living for all members (regardless of their true abilities). I'm talking about doctors, professors, lawyers, etc.

Today we are witnessing a Cambrian explosion of professions and specializations. We have dog surf instructors, professional coders (people queuing for you), fortune cookie writers, and many others. I have deliberately chosen examples of funny and absurd professions but just look at the new job positions open on LinkedIn to get an idea of how much the world of work has really changed.

If it is true, however, that specialization niches have exploded in number, it is equally true that only people perceived as the undisputed references in these micro-sectors are truly successful in the individual niches. These people, leveraging their personal brand, are able to attract the best bargains even without looking for them. In other words, thanks to their uniqueness and recognizability, it is lucky to find these people. These three forms of luck are sequential. This means that we don't have to put the cart before the horse, and to start getting luckier, we must first increase our chances of success thanks to pure and simple commitment.

THE RIGHT MOMENT

For years, Andrea Bocelli, the famous opera singer, had been told by music critics that he would never break through. In singing, either you are successful as a young man, or it's too late. He didn't give a damn, and in 1999, after five albums with poor sales, he released *Sacred Arias*. With 5 million copies sold, it became the best-selling classical music solo album of all time. At the time, Bocelli was 41 years old. The year 1993, JK Rowling, the author of the successful Harry Potter saga, recently returned to Edinburgh, Scotland. She had just separated, was unemployed, and had a dependent daughter. In the following years, she lived on state subsidies and odd jobs. In her spare time, however, she tried to keep her head busy with the writing of her fictional novel for children. She finished it in 1995, but the book was rejected by eleven different publishing houses. In 1997, London's Bloomsbury decided to give her a chance, publishing a skimpy first edition of only 1,000 copies. They sold like hot cakes. From that moment on, the adventures of the most famous wizard in the world became an international literary phenomenon. Rowling was well past her 30s in those days.

Ferruccio Lamborghini was an impetuous man with an iron will. After the war, he managed to create a good brand, thanks to his farm tractors, but he was still not satisfied. In 1963, he founded the "Lamborghini Automobile" and created a super sports car to compete with the much more famous and noble Ferrari. They called him crazy and said things like, "It will be a black hole for your finances! You will end up eating all your money for this extravagance!" and "Stay where you are, building tractors." In the same year, the Lamborghini 350 GTV, a work of art in both looks and mechanics, was shown at the Turin Motor Show. Then you all know the story. Ferruccio had just turned 47 years old.

Each of us lives our lives in our own personal time bubble, and there is no rule that prevents us from finding the right moment—our right time.

WEEKEND

I recently read a sentence that I found particularly interesting. The sentence goes thus, "Use the weekend to build the life you want instead of trying to escape the life you have"— Jari Roomer.

"Using the weekend to build the life we want" does not in any way mean that we have to work on the weekend as well, or at least it doesn't just mean that. Of course, if we are engaged in a job that pays our bills during the week but we want to launch our own project, it will be natural to work on several Saturdays and Sundays for a certain period of our life. I did, and I am grateful for it. But most importantly, "using the weekend" also means, above all, exploring new hobbies and passions instead of getting lost in the usual alienating distractions.

Finally, it is important to understand that there is a huge difference between "distraction" and "regeneration," on the other hand. I will never get tired of repeating it. Many people are convinced that "breaking up on the weekend" or abandoning oneself to distractions is synonymous with relaxation, but anyone who plays sports, loves being in the midst of nature, or has a real passion knows that a weekend of "intense adventure" is much more regenerating. Spend the weekend sprawled on the sofa. Ok, clarify these points; if the phrase I shared resonated with you, here is the simplest action you can take now to "use your weekend to build the life you want."

Of course, this action in itself will not be enough to help you realize your dreams, but it is the first step. On Sunday in the late afternoon or evening, take 15 minutes on the clock and plan the coming week. Choose the personal and professional activities you intend to carry out, decide when to practice the healthy habits you want to establish, and note the appointments you cannot miss.

BE YOURSELF

I recently happened to read a comment on a post that went more or less like this. "Why follow these directions? We have to be ourselves!" Yes, "be ourselves" are two words that can be said almost effortlessly but carry a lot of weight and power. It's one of those wildcard phrases that automatically proves you right when used in any discussion! "To be ourselves." But what exactly does it mean to say that we must "be ourselves?" Have you ever taken the time to ponder this at all?

Does a few-month-old baby who cannot yet walk or eat on his own betray himself when he learns new skills and evolves? What about an extremely shy and insecure person who perhaps would like to open up to new experiences and acquire greater self-esteem? Should we stop him at all costs, imposing the diktat of "you must be yourself?"

A hundred other examples come to mind, and each of them makes me reflect on the fact that the rhetoric of being oneself is foolish and wrong, as well as the daughter of the worst static mentality.

The truth is that there is a huge unexpressed potential in each of us. These potentials vary, including physical potential, mental potential, and emotional potential.

Telling a person "you have to be yourself", is like telling a caterpillar that it has to keep crawling instead of turning into a butterfly. I find it much more inspiring to say to myself and to those who read me, "Strive every day to become your real you, the one that slumbers among your as yet unexpressed genes." I believe that is a better approach to expressing this point.

15 SECONDS

A few weeks ago, there was a problem with the electricity grid, and there was a power failure in the house for a couple of hours. As soon as I got back, of course, the various digital clocks went off, including that of the microwave oven. Nothing serious. What happened in the following days, however, made me reflect.

Every morning, when I went to the kitchen to make breakfast, I saw that the clock was flashing with the time still out of order due to the power cut. I looked at it and thought to myself: "Ah man, I have to fix it. Come on." Then I'll start and, of course, forget about it. This has been going on for at least ten days, and during that time, the digital clock flashed.

Every time I saw it again (at least 4-5 times a day), it ended up sucking a little bit of my attention in the following minutes. In the end, I decided to fix it, and out of curiosity, I timed myself for just 15 seconds. It took me 15 seconds to fix something that at least distracted my attention for a total of 30–40 minutes from the day I noticed the problem. But how many times have you found yourself in a similar situation too? Or maybe you are finding yourself right now?

There is that email in your inbox for weeks that you should be replying to, and that makes you anxious every time you see it. There is that administrative issue that you have to deal with, but you keep postponing. There is that Whatsapp message from that acquaintance you have yet to reply to for days.

We all have these little open loops in our lives. Taken individually, they are foolish and of secondary importance. Yet, they are there in our retro thoughts, and even if irrelevant, the more we let them accumulate and drag them over time, the more mental and emotional resources they drain us.

We shouldn't be surprised if we find it hard to concentrate and don't find the time (and energy) to carry on what really matters.

So, here is my personal growth idea:

As soon as you have finished reading this page, write down a list of all these small activities you have pending. They must be tasks that you can solve in 10 minutes or less. Put them in writing, no matter how insignificant they appear to be.

Now that you have your nice list of "open loops," start from the top one and start closing them one after the other.

THE CROOKED MIRROR

Almost every day, I drive the same way home. At a certain point on the road, I arrive at a slightly narrow intersection where before turning left, it is necessary to look at a parabolic mirror on the other side of the road. If I don't see cars coming from the opposite side in the mirror, I can pass. One day, I arrived at that intersection and the mirror—probably due to a strong storm that had occurred the night before—had turned and become useless. I drove a little farther with the car into the street, and after looking left and right, I passed.

I said to myself, "Damn, it's dangerous. Who knows when they'll fix it?"

The following day, always arriving at the same intersection, I find the same problem, and little by little, I pass again. On the third day, the same, and I said to myself, "Is it possible that nobody notices it? Is it possible that the sheriff never comes through here?"

I do not deny that I spent several days at that intersection, and the crooked mirror was always there. Once, I also promised myself that, when I got home, I would call the town hall to report it, but then I forgot about it.

For the umpteenth time, when I arrived at the intersection, I again found the mir ror was wrong; I pulled over to the right, got out, crossed the street, and turned the mirror. A screw of those that were close at hand had loosened; that's why it kept turning on its axis. I oriented the parable in the right direction and closed the screw. Time lost: 1 minute.

When I got back into the car, I realized how stupid I had been the previous two days.

I was waiting for the sheriff, the town hall, someone when, actually, the mirror needed me. I was that someone who hadn't shot it yet.

Even if that little breakdown gave me personal discomfort on a daily basis, I kept waiting for someone else to think about it. In reality, I could have intervened immediately, but the internal cage was not yet open, and custom still ruled over reason.

And has that ever happened to you? Did you act, or did you wait? How long have you waited for someone to turn your mirror over?

THE THREE ALTERNATIVES

Faced with a problem, we have three alternatives, which are all listed below.

Finding a culprit "Outsourcing" our problems is certainly the easiest way to deal with them and, indeed, to avoid them. In fact, it is the path chosen by most people. All their ills always have a clear culprit: the boss, the government, the family, the crisis, the pandemic, inflation, etc. Everyone can take the blame, just as long as it is not themselves. The problem is that as long as we keep blaming other people for our problems, we make it hard for ourselves to deal with and solve them.

Okay, that person was rude to you? OK. You suffered a clear injustice? OK. Bureaucracy makes your life impossible? OK. But what do YOU want to do right now? Taking full responsibility for your life is tough, really tough, but it gives you incredible power. Never give it to the offenders on duty.

We find something to distract us. If every time you have to deal with something difficult, tiring, or demanding, your automatic reaction is to distract yourself or procrastinate, then it means that "escape" is the behavioral strategy you have internalized to deal with your problems. The problem with this, however, is that problems don't resolve themselves when we choose to postpone them or hide them in some social media feed. In fact, they tend to grow larger: their shadow, or the stress and fear they project on our minds, grows larger. But their size also becomes bigger. That is the work we will have to do to solve them definitively. Ask yourself what problems you are avoiding facing when you obsessively search for distractions.

You need courage and focus to face a situation or a problem. Courage is needed because dealing with ourselves and with complex situations that do not have a clear solution can be frightening, demotivating, and stressful. Focus is needed because certain problems do not disappear suddenly but require an intense and continuous commitment on our part, and if we waste our energies on useless distractions or witch hunts, we will not have enough to escape safely from the storm.

Which of these three strategies are you adopting to face the challenges of your life, and which one do you choose to adopt from now on?

CONCLUSION

Greatness is not just achieved; it can also be learned and taught. It only happens that although there are so many places with information on how to achieve that state where you begin to maximize life to achieve results, there are only just a few results to show for the viability of this information. If you are reading this, it means that you have successfully flipped through the pages of this book and then gotten yourself to the very end of it.

Without a doubt, this act is worthy of applause and commendation. This book has been able to emphasize many of the points required for you to achieve everything you wish. In a world that seems to be littered with so much information, what is actually needed is to have at your disposal the right information that will not only occupy space in you and subsequently become garbage and a burden to you, but information as well as host the power to translate into palpable results for you, and this is exactly what this book promises. Beyond simply reading, you must commit to taking note of each of the tips shared throughout its pages and putting them into practice because it is only in this way that you can be certain of getting results from them.

Importantly, if you have read this book and you have found it very helpful, then the next appropriate thing to do is to share it with someone else who will also potentially find it helpful. Remember, it starts with you but doesn't end with you. Keep the train moving and also be a part of this movement simply by sharing it with others. See you on the other side of greatness.

Visit the author at www.saturneditors.com/bradmeier

RECOMMENDED BOOKS

- *How to Treat Others and Make Friends* - Dale Carnegie.
- *The 7 Rules to Succeed* - Stephen R. Covey.
- *The slight edge* - Jeff Olson.
- *Think and enrich yourself* - Napoleon Hill.
- *Psychocybernetics* - Maxwell Maltz.
- *Highway to Wealth* - MJ DeMarco.
- *The monk who sold his Ferrari* - Robin Sharma.
- *The Way of the Peace Warrior* - Dan Millman.
- *The Power of Now* - Eckhart Tolle.
- *4 hours a week* - Tim Ferriss.
- *Emotional Intelligence* - Daniel Goleman.
- *Quiet* - Susan Cain.
- *One thing only* - Gary Keller.
- *Straight to the point* - Greg McKeown.
- *The 12 week year* - Brian P. Moran.
- *The 4 disciplines of Execution* - Sean Covey.
- *The power of full engagement* - Tony Schwartz.
- *Deep work* - Cal Newport.
- *The 80/20 Principle* - Richard Koch.
- *Smartcuts* - Shane Snow.
- *Said, done* - David Allen.

- *My whole life* - Arnold Schwarzenegger.
- *Put out the fire of anger* - Thich Nhat Hanh.
- *Hagakure. The secret book of the samurai* - Yamamoto Tsunetomo.
- *The subtle art of not giving a f * ck* - Mark Manson.
- *The obstacle is the way* - Ryan Holiday.
- *Letters to Lucilius* - Seneca.
- *The seagull Johnatan Livingston* - Richard Bach.
- *Walden or life in the woods* - Henry David Thoreau.
- *So good they can't ignore you* - Cal Newport.
- *The dictatorship of habits* - Charles Duhigg.
- *The art of learning* - Josh Waitzkin.
- *The defining decade* - Mag Jay.
- *Money: Dominate the Game* - Tony Robbins.

Printed in Great Britain
by Amazon

11054834R00075